P9-DEA-168

RENEWED BY THE WORD

In loving memory of
Diana Morris 1928–1998

Renewed by the Word

The Bible and Christian Revival Since the Reformation

J. N. Morris

Renewed by the Word
Hendrickson Publishers,Inc.
P.O.Box 3473
Peabody, Massachusetts 01961-3473

The Bothy, Deershot Lodge, Park Lane, Ropley, Hants, SO24 0BE, UK
Tel: +44 (0) 1962 773768 Fax: +44 (0) 1962 773769
E-mail: office@johnhunt-publishing.com
www.johnhunt-publishing.com
www.0-books.net

UK ISBN 1 842981 47 1
US ISBN 1 56563 533 7

Concept: Robert Dudley, Bowerdean Publishing
Design: Mousemat Design Limited, Kent, UK
Except where credited, pictures are from private collections or from Art Today

Printed by Maple-Vail Ltd, USA

Contents

Introduction

THE CHRISTIAN CHURCH comes in many different forms today. Sometimes it seems as if there are almost as many different Christian churches as there are Christian people. There is a huge diversity of languages spoken by Christians, of forms of worship used, of structures of organization, and of interpretations of belief. This diversity is not a recent phenomenon. It has been long in the making. It leaves us often bewildered at the apparent variety of choice on offer to the practicing Christian today. Yet Christianity in the modern world has also been fashioned by certain common experiences. One of the most powerful and vibrant of these has been revivalism. Much of what we experience and value in the modern Christian churches has been shaped by a movement of renewal that can be traced back into the early years of the modern era. In order to understand how the churches in America and Britain are as they are today, we need to review that history, and to trace its origins. Yet we must never suppose that this is a lifeless inquiry. The need of the Church to seek revival, to renew itself, comes from the very nature of the convictions that called it into being in the first place. *That* is where we have to begin.

Jesus Christ as the center of history

Right from the very beginning, Christians were faced with a strange and perplexing mystery about the origins of their faith. When Jesus Christ was raised from the dead, as they believed, it was no longer possible to think of him as living only a historical existence. He had been born, lived, and died. Thus far, his life was like all other lives. True, he had performed miracles. He had also made astonishing claims for himself, claims that apparently shocked some of the religious leaders of his day. He was killed because of this. Yet even those closest to him, those who heard his teaching and lived with him as he went round the villages of Galilee proclaiming his message, were confused about who he really was. According to the Gospel of Mark, when Jesus asked his disciples who people thought he was, they said John the Baptist, or Elijah, or "one of the prophets." But only Peter said, "You are the Christ," that is, the anointed savior. And when Jesus then began to tell them about his coming death and resurrection, even Peter rebuked him for it. It was extraordinarily difficult to see Jesus in any other way than as a human being, however wise, who would die just like anyone else. It is no wonder that, in the days after his crucifixion, his followers were disconsolate, and hid. They had no real faith that Jesus would, after all, rise again.

But all that changed with the resurrection. Now, Jesus had passed beyond the known limits of human existence. Just what he was, and who he was, became a source of wonder and inspiration for his followers. Now they began to see his earthly ministry in a new way. More than they could possibly have done before, they saw God's presence in him. Jesus, ascending into heaven, reassured them that he would be with them in the future. Matthew's Gospel ends with Jesus commissioning his disciples for their future task, and reassuring them of his presence: "Go ye therefore, and teach all nations, baptizing them in the name of the Father, and of the Son, and of the Holy Ghost: teaching them to observe all things whatsoever I have commanded you: and lo, I am with you always, even unto the end of the world."

Were those words to be heard and understood only by the circle of Jesus' immediate followers? Surely not. Surely those who heard them, recited perhaps in the meetings of fellowship that began not long after Jesus' ascension, would have thought they were of lasting significance. They applied to all who followed Jesus. They marked out a special course of action for the Christian community: take my gospel to the world, teach and baptize whoever you can, live as I have urged you to live, and be confident that I am with you wherever and whenever you do this.

"Take my Gospel to the world". The descent of the Holy Ghost at Pentecost by El Greco

Since God was in Jesus Christ, as Christians believed, wherever the living Christ was, there God could be found. God could be approached through faith in the living Jesus Christ, because to believe in him as living was to believe in his resurrection. For the Christian community, life was now centered on a savior who was eternally present. In one sense, Jesus became the center of history for Christians. St Paul saw very clearly that Jesus' salvation of humankind, through his death and resurrection, marked the end of one period of history that had begun with the fall of Adam and Eve, and the beginning of a new history, a new time of hope and promise. Paul accepted the tradition that death was a consequence of the Fall, but proclaimed its defeat through Jesus Christ: "[S]ince by man came death, by man came also the resurrection of the dead. For as in Adam all die, even so in Christ shall all be made alive."

But the Jesus who was a historical person also became, for Christians, a person who rose above history, who remained ever-present for them. Their faith, as it developed and eventually grew away from Judaism, held on to a double truth. Jesus had once lived on earth, and his actions and words then remained of absolute significance for his followers. They were remembered in preaching and in letter-writing, they were recorded in the lives that have come down to us as the four Gospels of Matthew, Mark, Luke, and John, and they were recalled in particular acts of worship. But Jesus was also with his followers eternally. He was prayed to, adored, imitated, and experienced as a living person.

So Jesus was the center of history, and also out of history. He had a historical existence – a birth, life, and death – and also an ever-present existence, a new life. The early Christians looked back to his life on earth, and built their worship and religious convictions around the events of that life, and yet they also were convinced that Jesus really was with them, a continual source of faith, hope, and love.

As time passed, these two convictions sometimes came into tension with each other. As the Christian Church grew, and changed, it had to become more organized. Arguments arose over what true belief entailed, over who Jesus really was, over the nature of God, and over the organization and authority of the Church. What had begun as a small, very informal movement of humble people became, over the centuries, an organization spread across virtually the whole of Europe, North Africa, and the Middle East. It became a hierarchical body, with clearly designated leaders, or bishops, and with priests and deacons and other orders ("minor orders") who led its local life. In time it created training institutions, the early universities. It developed special religious communities within its own ranks, the religious orders, bound together by special oaths of poverty, celibacy, and obedience, and practices of discipline. It even developed its own system of law – "canon law" – with ecclesiastical courts to administer it. None of this represented an abandonment of the spirit and word of Jesus Christ. In fact, to Christians then, as to many now, it was merely a logical development and expansion of the early Christian Church, a necessary accommodation to protect the spirit and word of Christ in the changing situation of history.

But intricate organization creates its own demands, because organizations have to be sustained by human effort, and yet it is not always easy to see just when one particular institutional practice or feature has ceased to be useful. Just as the Christian Church has always had to find a way of adjusting to changing circumstance, so that the gospel of salvation through Jesus Christ can be proclaimed in every age, so Christians have disagreed with each other over what adjustment was necessary, and when and how. Sometimes they have failed to see that radical new solutions were necessary. Sometimes they have resisted change bitterly, only to see new groups arise to challenge the old ways. Sometimes the old ways have survived, and then flourished in new situations.

Yet at each of these crucial points of change, which have been many in the history of the Christian Church, the conviction that Jesus Christ was ever-present to his followers has been an inspiration to them. It has been so, both to those who resisted change and to those who advocated it. From within itself, the Church has sponsored renewal ceaselessly. Christians could look back to the earthly life of Jesus, and to the historical events of his birth, death, and resurrection, and see themselves as a blessed people. They could value the heritage of worship, law, and tradition that the Christian Church had created over the centuries. Yet sometimes this very heritage could become a straitjacket. Then, new movements could arise that took their inspiration from the belief that Jesus – *their* Lord and Master – was with them now, guiding them and leading them into new ways. These new insights, and new practices or forms of organization, sometimes came into direct conflict with older, established patterns of Christian life and belief, and caused division and even war.

Sometimes they led to internal renewal, avoiding open conflict but equipping the Church to adapt and survive in ever-changing circumstances. Whatever the outcome, Christians rediscovered Jesus in their own lives. In new, often unforeseen ways, his everlasting presence with them gave them new hope.

The possibility of endless renewal, which comes from this tension between the belief that Jesus was a historical person who lived and died in first-century Palestine and the faith that this same Jesus lives still and is with his followers, has given Christianity a dynamic, restless spirit. Christian churches have often become trapped by too great an attachment to their inherited traditions, vital though these are. They have stagnated, and faltered in their mission. But they have also been open to renewal. The history of the Church as a whole, on a long view, looks like a succession of periods of growth, consolidation, and apparent decline, punctured by waves of revival.

Luther preaching

Revivalism in the modern world

Like all great movements of ideas, Christianity has taken shape in time through absorbing and transforming elements of the culture in which it has taken root. At first, this happened in a piecemeal way. Christians were persecuted in the Roman Empire, and were very much a minority. But when Christianity became the official religion of the Empire, and in time spread throughout western Europe and the Mediterranean area, it became impossible to separate the Church altogether from the culture it inhabited. Society became Christianized. Then, the movements of renewal that flooded through the Church from time to time developed out of familiar features of Christian culture. The religious orders in particular were a model for those seeking to renew the Church's mission. In the conversion of northern Europe, monks were the missionaries, bound together in a close bond of loyalty to the Pope, and sharing a common discipline. Later, in more settled times, the orders of friars – especially the Franciscans and Dominicans – sought to renew the Church from within.

But the greatest movement of renewal in the West was also the most divisive – the Reformation. Though it began as a movement within the medieval Church (Luther himself was a friar), it soon engineered a permanent split in the Church. Thereafter, within what came to be called the Protestant churches, renewal could not come from the same source as had happened in earlier ages, since the religious orders had been suppressed. Now, in time, movements of revival came to demonstrate features of the rapidly changing societies in which they were situated. Since we live in a world we call "modern," these were recognizably "modern" features. Revivalism thrived on the opportunities of mass communication opened up by printing. It involved the summoning of mass meetings. It often demonstrated the influence of individualism and

St Dominic – founder of the Dominican Order

democratic views, with new opportunities for leadership and organization open to lay people. Revivalist leaders could use the new forms of transport – improved roads and carriages, canals, railways – to carry their message far and wide. Exploration, and the opening up of the New World of the Americas, in turn provided a rich field of missionary endeavor.

The French Revolution galvanised the Roman Catholic Church

Revivalism in the modern age came to mean something quite specific. Identified as a movement within Protestantism, it came to mean the use of techniques of mass organization and leadership, and emotional stimulation centering on repentance and dramatic conversion, to transform the faith of apparently lukewarm Christians, and to increase the number of converts. This is the main subject of this book. But we must not forget that revival is a recurrent aspect of Christian history, affecting all branches of the Christian Church – not just Protestantism. And in Roman Catholicism in particular, there have been echoes of Protestant revivalism. Thus, revivalism can help us to understand something of the history of our modern world, because it has developed in and through the rise of modern society, and it has thrived on the use of what are essentially modern techniques of organization and communication. Yet it can also help us to understand something of the history of the Christian churches as a whole in America and Britain, since it has affected all the main branches of

Modern Protestantism was much influenced by the "Great Awakening" (Photograph © Getty Images)

Christianity here. It is like a telescope through which we can look at key events and people in the modern history of Christianity.

When we look through that telescope at the modern world, what we see essentially are three main waves of revival. Starting in the middle of the eighteenth century, and running on into the nineteenth century, in Britain and America we see the first, the "Evangelical" revival. Called the "Great Awakening" in the first phase in America, this was a great outburst of renewed missionary zeal and confidence, emotionally intense and restless. It transformed the Protestant churches on both sides of the Atlantic. Though there were periods of greater and lesser intensity within it, and though in America it is customary to speak of a "Second Awakening" in the early nineteenth century, it is really one great period of renewal, the effects of which are still very much with us. Modern Protestantism in so many ways was made by this great Evangelical revival.

The second wave was Catholic. From the early nineteenth century, galvanized by the catastrophic effect of the French Revolution and the Napoleonic Wars on the Catholic Church in Europe, by migration of Irish and then Mediterranean peoples to America, by the new industrial cities, and by the rapid development of the American frontier, the Catholic Church echoed many of the features of Evangelical Protestantism – its enthusiasm, its use of mass meetings, its organization – in order to reassert its position in the modern world. Catholic revivalism of course was distinctive, as we shall see, but again its effects are very much with us still, in the shape and culture of the Catholic churches it created in Britain and America. It lasted well into the twentieth century.

But by then new and distinct emphases were emerging once again in Protestantism. Sharing much with the older forms of Evangelicalism, Pentecostalism nevertheless represented a new and startling development of it. The rediscovery of charismatic gifts, such as prophecy and speaking in tongues, gave rise to very different forms of worship and church life from those common in the older Evangelical churches. New denominations came into being. The Pentecostal, or charismatic, revival, is also still with us. It has released extraordinary energy among Protestant Christians. Pentecostalism is growing rapidly not just in North America, but especially in Latin America, in Africa, and the East. It has effected a global transformation in Christianity, with growth now occurring most spectacularly outside the European and American churches that for so long have claimed to lead world Christianity. Its impact has spread to the older churches, including the Catholic churches. It has encouraged there the adoption of new musical styles, new forms of preaching, and new styles of worship. It may yet have a long way to run. Its future development is unknown. Seen by some as a flight from the modern world, and by others as typically modern, its ultimate effect on the Christian faith has yet to be decided.

The Bible and the modern world

If it is the conviction that Jesus Christ is with them still that has inspired Christians in successive periods of renewal, what has given specific shape to these movements of renewal? It is above all the Bible. What Christians know about Jesus and his gospel of salvation they know through the Bible. The ultimate authority for Christians in all matters of dispute is the Bible. The ultimate source of knowledge of God for Christians is the Bible. Jesus, described in John's Gospel as the Word, meets us in the text of Scripture that is also the Word of God. Christians have drawn great insight from other sources, including the history and traditions of the Church, human reason, and human experience. The significance of these things in Christian history should never be underestimated. But they have always had to be received in relation to the truth Christians have seen in Scripture.

This is not to suggest that what Scripture has to say has always been self-evident to Christians. It needs interpretation to be received afresh in each age. As the centuries have passed since the Scriptures were written, Christians have been confronted time and again with new questions that were not explicitly answered in the Bible. There have been – and still are – wide areas of dispute about what the Bible is saying to us. To what extent can we say the Bible is inspired? What kind of truth is to be encountered in the Word of God? Is it literal truth? Or is it metaphorical? Or is it both? Or is it, perhaps, sometimes literal, sometimes metaphorical, sometimes narrative, sometimes legal, and so on? Can we distinguish between basic, essential commands, and things that are inessential? There are no easy answers to these questions. The possibility of disagreement between Christians is great. Differences of interpretation have run through Christian history, and driven conflict between Christians.

The fact of conflict has to be acknowledged. Yet what is striking is the willingness of Christians again and again to re-root their faith in Scripture. The

Bible lies at the very center of the great movements of church history. Through its sacred texts, Christians encountered again and again the Christ of their faith. The Bible was at once a fearfully authoritative book, and an intensely personal one. It gave a worldwide institution, the Church, the norms that became embedded in a great system of law. Yet it was a book for every person. In reading or hearing its words, and reflecting on them in their hearts, Jesus of Nazareth came to inhabit the faith of ordinary people.

THE
HOLY
BIBLE,
Conteyning the Old Testament,
AND THE NEW:
Newly Translated out of the Originall
tongues: & with the former Translations
diligently compared and revised by his
Maiesties speciall Comandement.
Appointed to be read in Churches.
Imprinted at London by Robert
Barker, Printer to the Kings
most Excellent Maiestie.
ANNO DOM. 1611

Title page from a Bible of 1611

The history of the Christian Church is the history of the people of the book of the Bible. The great waves of revivalism that have made the churches of our world were inspired by these ancient texts, these living witnesses to the history of the savior who walked in Palestine, and lived and died and rose again for humankind. Tracing the story of these great movements of revival, we are tracing the story of ordinary Christians' passion for the Bible.

Chapter 1

WARS OF RELIGION

OUR STORY IS revivalism in the modern world. But its beginning lies farther back than the eighteenth century. To understand the nature of this movement of renewal within Protestantism, we have to grasp something of the origins of Protestantism itself.

At the beginning of the sixteenth century, if you lived in western Europe, you could be forgiven for thinking that Christianity had reached its greatest moment. The Christian empire of the papacy stretched from Scandinavia in the north to Spain and Italy in the south, from Ireland in the west to Poland in the east. In this great swathe of kingdoms, the one Church of Christ owed allegiance to its one visible head, the Pope, who sat on the throne of St Peter in Rome. True, it was not an empire in any conventional sense. The language of empire was used rarely. "Christendom" is the word now used commonly to describe medieval Europe. The Pope claimed the allegiance of all temporal rulers, princes, and kings within this area, but his power was severely limited in practice. Few rulers gave him much scope to interfere practically with the government of their lands. The Church, however, was a great landowner, wealthy in its own right, and powerful by virtue of its near-monopoly of learning. It mingled with the great, raised armies for princes, and supplied civil servants for monarchs. To the east of this Christian Europe, the Eastern, Greek-speaking churches looked with suspicion on their western Catholic neighbors. Attempts to heal the breach between the western, Latin Church and the eastern Church had failed finally at the Council of Florence in 1438 to 1445. To the south and south-east, dominating much of the Mediterranean Sea, lay the lands of Islam. The Moors had been driven out of Spain finally in the late fifteenth century, but the Turks had seized Constantinople in 1453, and with its fall the Byzantine Empire, with its Greek-speaking church, had finally come to an end.

Medieval Christendom in fact was not so much a single polity, as a loose federation of kingdoms and principalities that looked for ecclesiastical guidance to Rome. Many of the linguistic communities of modern Europe were already well on their way to coming into being. The realm of the English-speaking peoples was a single nation under one monarch. Scotland was an independent state. France had also come to occupy something like its present geographical area. The lands of the German-speaking peoples in central Europe were held by a host of different princes, yet some theoretical coherence was given to them by their inclusion in the Holy Roman Empire. All these lands had their own customs, their own systems of law, their own distinct histories. Yet, despite this diversity, the unity of medieval Christendom was also evident. One language – Latin – made communication between church leaders and rulers across Europe relatively easy. Ecclesiastical bureaucracy stretched a chain of connections across Europe, crossing national or territorial boundaries. Local disputes involving the Church, and sometimes even non-ecclesiastical disputes, might be taken to Rome for final adjudication. The fact of a common faith did not stop Europe's rulers and nobles from indulging in the usual cycles of territorial ambition and war. But the Pope's claim to authority was very great. In 1198 Pope Innocent III even argued that "the moon derives her light from the sun, and is in truth inferior to the sun … In the same way the royal power derives its dignity from the pontifical authority."[1] Though this claim never gained

St Peter's Rome

universal acceptance, and was in any case damaged by the papacy's own divisions in the fourteenth and fifteenth centuries, the Pope remained a powerful figure in European politics.

Yet these bonds of ecclesiastical unity burst apart in the early sixteenth century. What became a social, political, and religious upheaval began almost mundanely, with an academic dispute between monks over the theology of penance. In the late medieval church, the possibility of performing acts of penance that could shorten your time in purgatory after death (and so speed you to heaven) gave rise to the controversial practice of selling "indulgences," or fixed periods of reduction of punishment. The building of the great basilica in Rome, St Peter's, begun toward the end of the fifteenth century, marked the visible authority and dignity of the papacy. Yet St Peter's was financed in part by the sale of indulgences. The Augustinian friar Martin Luther (1483–1546) questioned the theology that justified this practice. His famous "Ninety-Five Theses" may not actually have been nailed to the door of the castle church in Wittenburg in 1517, but their impact was immense. The need for reform of the Church had been debated hotly for decades, and starting a discussion on this was hardly original. But Luther's challenge was novel in its force and in its implications. It set in train an argument about the theology of penance, and in turn the authority of the papacy, that has never been laid to rest since then. Local rulers took sides on the matter. The dispute snowballed. The Reformation, as it was later called, engineered a permanent division in the Christian Church. Within forty years, much of northern Europe had embraced the new theological insights of the Reformers – men such as Martin Luther himself, Philipp Melancthon, Ulrich Zwingli, Martin Bucer, and John Calvin. Much of southern Europe remained faithful to the papacy. But this was never a neat and tidy division.

John Calvin

The Castle at Wittenburg

There was a great deal of overlap, a great deal of confusion. In all countries, dissenting minorities came into being, whether Catholic in the new Protestant realms, or Protestant (of various shades of opinion) in Catholic countries.

At the heart of this fundamental division in the western Church lay the Bible. Influenced by "Humanist" scholars (so called centuries later, because of their concern to advance the study of the human sciences through the revival of classical learning) such as the Dutchman Desiderius Erasmus, the Reformers looked afresh at the traditional way of using and interpreting the Bible. What they found dissatisfied them. The traditional emphasis of Catholic practice had been on the role of the educated clergy as interpreters of the Scriptures. Mostly, the Bible was not made available to lay people in their own languages, but was used in a Latin version (the "Vulgate") dating back to the fourth century. A devotional life shaped by the Church was assumed to be the only context within which the Bible could be read. In effect, this made the Church the only true interpreter of the Bible, and the Church's authority was made visible and effective through the hierarchy of the clergy. The Reformers came to see things in a quite different way. The Church had to be evaluated (and reformed) in the light of the Bible. Since the Bible was the inspired Word of God, it must stand over and above any human agency, however impressive and powerful that agency might be. As Luther argued, "When the pope acts contrary to the Scriptures, it is our duty to stand by the Scriptures, to reprove him and constrain him, according to the word of Christ."[2] The Christian life was to be discerned through the sole and supreme authority of the Bible – "by Scripture alone," or *sola scriptura*, in the Latin (as Latin continued to be used as the language of scholarly dispute among Protestants for a hundred years). The Reformers' conviction was of the freedom of the ordinary person to hear and receive the Word of God. This remained central to Protestantism, and lies behind much of the force of later Evangelical religion. Through the recent invention of printing, and through encouraging translations of the Bible into the ordinary languages of Europe, the

Reformers claimed to put the Bible back into the hands of ordinary believers. William Tyndale first began to translate the Bible into English in the 1520s, but had to do so in exile in Germany, because at that time the English Church had not separated from Rome.

William Tyndale

But the Reformers were concerned not only with the question of *who* was able to read the Bible. They were also concerned with *what* was read, or rather with what could be found in it. The medieval method of interpretation had conceived of a number of overlapping senses in which the text could be read. As well as attending to the literal sense of a passage, the medieval Christian could consider what allegorical meaning might be found in it, or what moral importance it might be seeking to convey. Passages might vary in the degree to which they could be read this way. Medieval commentaries on the Bible took their lead from the early traditions of the Christian Church, and interpreted the Scriptures particularly in that light. In that way, they could use the Bible creatively and imaginatively to justify features of Church life, organization, and doctrine that were not obviously present in the literal sense of the text. St Augustine, one of the great teachers of the early Christian Church, famously used the passionate, even erotic imagery of the Song of Songs as an allegory of Christ's love for his Church. This was anathema to the Reformers. They came to stress what we might call the "plain sense" of Scripture. It was not to be read allegorically or metaphorically, but with simple, faithful attention to what it actually said. As Luther said against his opponents, "They expound and proclaim the

Scriptures! But if the Scripture they proclaim is obscure, who will assure us that their proclamation is dependable?" And he went on, "If Scripture is obscure or equivocal, why need it have been brought down to us by act of God? Surely we have enough obscurity and uncertainty within ourselves, without our obscurity and uncertainty and darkness being augmented from heaven!"[3]

Now we should be very careful not to fall into the trap of thinking that Protestants were "for" the Bible, and Catholics "against" it. There were plenty of church people who remained faithful to Rome who yet encouraged the study of the Bible. The Bible has always been at the very center of Catholic Christianity. The argument, finally, concerned authority. The Reformers saw themselves as freeing the Bible from the artificial restraints put upon it by the late medieval Church. They did not think of themselves as revolutionaries. They thought they were simply returning the Scriptures to their proper use, and making them freely available to all. They did not want to encourage a confusing babble of conflicting interpretations, as their opponents alleged. They thought the meaning of Scripture was plain enough. If all people could read the Bible, and hear it read aloud in their own language, and preached clearly, then the truth of the gospel – the truth of the salvation and justification wrought by Jesus Christ – would be evident. This was not intended to be an attack on all church authority. But it was, on the other hand, giving ordinary lay people much greater freedom to learn for themselves what their faith involved. We can catch something of the excitement of this from the prologue to William Tyndale's translation of the Pentateuch, the first five books of the Old Testament, in 1530:

> Though a man had a precious jewel and a rich, yet if he wist [knew] not the value thereof nor wherefore it served, he were neither the better nor richer of a straw. Even so though we read the scripture and babble of it never so much, yet if we know not the use of it, and

> wherefore [why] it was given, and what is therein to be sought, it profiteth us nothing at all. It is not enough therefore to read and talk of it only, but we must also desire God day and night instantly to open our eyes, and to make us understand and wherefore the scripture was given that we may apply the medicine of scripture, every man to his own sores.[4]

Religious conflict

The division of Europe into competing versions of Christianity was a much more dangerous matter than we might think today. In our world, in America and Europe, on the whole our societies have become accustomed to living with religious difference. We call this religious pluralism. We might have very serious disagreements over particular things, but mostly we are prepared to recognize that people with very different religious opinions from us are entitled to some freedom to express their views, and to some protection under the law (as long as they obey the law). This was not the case at all in the sixteenth century. Even after the main events of the Reformation in Europe, on the whole Christians continued to assume that there could be only one acceptable form of religious expression. The social imagination of people was not pluralist. It was the duty of rulers to promote religious truth, because social stability depended on it. Catholics and Protestants alike believed in God's providential ordering of the world. The sins of groups of people, up to and including whole nations, might be punished by catastrophe such as war, pestilence, and famine. Heresy was a sin. So was schism. For a hundred and fifty years or more after the beginning of the Reformation, Christians throughout Europe were busy searching the signs of the times for evidence of God's favor or God's judgment.

They were also busy fighting over religion. In southern Europe, in Spain and Italy, Protestant minorities were never very significant, and it was relatively easy for Catholic rulers to suppress or contain them. In France, a sizeable Protestant community came into being in the course of the sixteenth century, and it took France a hundred years to manage the ensuing social and religious divisions, through civil war, attempted toleration, massacre (for example, the infamous St Bartholomew's day massacre of thousands of Huguenots, French Protestants, in Paris and other French cities in 1572), and finally suppression, with exile, of the Protestants. At the end of the sixteenth century, it looked as if France would be a permanently divided State. By the end of the seventeenth century, Protestantism had virtually disappeared from France. In northern Europe, in Scandinavia and the Baltic states, on the contrary consolidated Lutheran national churches were formed, and Catholic communities were dispersed, persecuted, or disappeared altogether. In central Europe, a complex pattern of changing religious allegiance on the part of rulers confused the picture for decades, but finally, in 1618, it all broke in the beginning of the savage Thirty Years' War. This was really a vicious series of mini-wars, which secured again for Catholicism much of central Europe, including parts of southern Germany, but confirmed (with Swedish help) the preservation of Protestant states in northern Germany. This was not only a religious conflict. Protestants did fight against Protestants on occasions, and Catholics against Catholics, especially in the last stages of the conflict when France entered the war on the side of Protestant Sweden. But the fundamental division of Europe into sharply opposed religious communities intensified the conflict immeasurably.

And what about Britain? The two kingdoms of England (including Wales and Ireland at this time) and Scotland seemed unable to live peaceably together. For the whole of the sixteenth century they maintained a separate existence. The Reformation came relatively late to Scotland, but when it did so, it came in a peculiarly intense and violent form. The reformed Church of Scotland came into being in 1560, but the monarch remained Catholic (and therefore a center of anti-Protestant support) until Mary I, better known as "Queen of Scots" was forced to abdicate in 1567, and was finally beheaded by her cousin Elizabeth, Queen of

England, in 1587. The Scottish Reformation, like the English by this time, came in the form not of Luther's theology, but of the more radical theology, later to be called variously "Reformed," "Presbyterian," or "Calvinist," of the way of the Reformation that followed ultimately the Frenchman Jean Calvin. Calvin's theology – put into practice in the Swiss city state of Geneva – added to Luther's work a more consistently developed doctrine of predestination. People were foreordained to eternal life – or not. It also rejected the traditional form of the ministry, of church organization, and ways of worshipping, much of which Luther had in fact accepted. This "Calvinist" theology, not Lutheranism, historically was the main reforming influence on England and Scotland.

Henry VIII

In England, the rejection of the Pope had happened mostly for political expediency. Henry VIII wanted a male heir. His wife Katherine of Aragon could not bear him one. Henry wanted to divorce her and marry Anne Boleyn instead. The Pope could not permit this. So Henry broke from the Pope and married Anne anyway. Henry remained a traditional Catholic, in many ways. His son, Edward VI, was not. In his reign England moved sharply toward a full Protestant Reformation. But Edward died young, and his Catholic sister Mary tried to reinstate Catholicism in England. Mary's reign, too, was short, and was followed by the long reign of her sister Elizabeth, a Protestant like her brother. Back and forth the attempt to settle religion had gone in England, causing confusion, protest, and rebellion. By the end of the sixteenth century, the Church of England, a Protestant church, was becoming more and more internally divided, between those who accepted the rather odd mix of traditional, Catholic organization (with bishops and cathedrals) and Protestant theology the Church had become, and the "Puritans" who wanted to reform it more drastically. After Elizabeth's death in 1603, childless as she was, England and Scotland were united under one ruler, James VI of Scotland, who became James I of England. In the middle of the seventeenth century, in the reign of James's unfortunate son, Charles I, religious rivalry burst into civil war. For nine years, the kingdoms were torn by war. Charles was executed by Parliament. England, and a reluctant Scotland, were declared a republic, under the military leader Oliver Cromwell.

And what of America? The European discovery of the "new world" was a late medieval phenomenon. After all, as the popular rhyme goes, it was in 1492 that "Columbus sailed the ocean blue." From then on, into the time of the Reformation and beyond, the Americas were rapidly opened up to European settlement. In this, the religious divisions of Europe were never far from the surface. In the Spanish and Portuguese colonies of central and southern America, Catholicism was established from the very beginning as the dominant form of Christianity. Local, original ("first American") religious cults were usually suppressed with some savagery, and

Columbus reaches the New World

conversion enforced. By the late sixteenth century, a few French colonies had been established on the northeastern seaboard, such as Sable Island, and Tadoussac. These were also predominantly Catholic. Later, the French moved inland, settling for example around what was eventually to become modern Quebec. As a result, a Catholic presence was established early in Canada. It was there, too, further south, in the colony of Maryland. But Maryland was a British colony, which happened to have a governor, Lord Baltimore, who was a convert to Catholicism. For a century or more, the pattern of settlement along the eastern coast of America was to reflect British expansionism. But also British religious division. The Pilgrim Fathers' flight from religious oppression in England, and their establishment of Plymouth in 1620, was symptomatic of this. So too was the settlement of other Puritans from England in Massachusetts in 1629. Further south, in 1607, the Virginia colony had been founded with the Church of England dominant. Yet the export of European religious division to America did not on the whole produce the bitter conflict that it had in

Europe itself. Why was this? It is hard not to conclude that there was a very simple explanation – the sheer size of America. The new colonies were often hundreds of miles apart. There was land enough for everyone – if the Native American inhabitants could be cajoled or persuaded to give it up. America soaked up incoming population for centuries, well into the twentieth century, like an enormous sponge, diluting the intensity of sectarian conflict as it did so.

Peace and toleration

Returning to Europe, by the end of the seventeenth century bitter religious division appeared to have burnt itself out. The Peace of Westphalia in 1648 brought to an end the Thirty Years' War, and did so by acknowledging the separate existence of permanent Protestant and Catholic churches in the central, mostly German states of Europe, those which made up the Holy Roman Empire. Now, where communities were religiously divided, the acceptance of the differences between Protestant and Catholic countries had come to be seen as a necessary condition of peace. Governments had given up on the ambition of achieving uniformity of religious practice in their realms. In most cases, states remained particularly supportive of one form of religion rather than another. The Latin phrase that described this settlement – *cuius regio, eius religio* ("whoever rules, his is the dominant religion") – captures the sense in which the sheer political diversity of Europe prevented each form of Christianity from suppressing the other altogether.

From the late seventeenth century until the early nineteenth century, central Europe was dominated by almost three hundred different states or principalities, some no larger than a single city, others large and expanding states, like Prussia. What was called the Holy Roman Empire was, as the French historian and philosopher Voltaire famously said, "Neither Holy, nor Roman, nor an Empire." It was nothing more than a loose agglomeration of territories. The sheer violence of the Thirty Years' War, and the desolation it had caused, emptied religion on both sides of the capacity to pull states together in a spirit of unity. The Catholic response to Protestantism, the "Counter-Reformation" (sometimes called the "Catholic Reformation") had imbued Catholicism with a new sense of purpose and resolve. But the papacy was evidently in decline, its ability to support and encourage Catholic monarchs in active defense of Catholicism practically spent. Now, rulers had to accept that religion could not act as the central, unifying force it had for centuries been assumed to be. Its political influence was diminished. Yet, in most of Europe, there were no emergent democratic movements to counter royal or princely power. As a result, across Europe by the end of the seventeenth century a new and much more centralized form of monarchy began to emerge – what historians have called "Enlightened despotism." In the states ruled by these absolutists, certain rights were often given to religious minorities to assemble and worship, though they were strictly limited. In that sense, there was a spirit of toleration abroad, though it was nothing like as extensive as our modern concept of toleration. In France, Spain, Austria, and other Catholic states, Protestants were persecuted or barely tolerated, and social and political criticism vigorously suppressed. Elsewhere, Catholics were grudgingly accepted, but often remained excluded from political office.

Charles I on his way to the scaffold

Britain was something of an

exception. Its society looked for all the world much like that of Europe as a whole. It had a hereditary aristocracy, who continued to wield immense influence, just as their social equals did on the continent of Europe. It had "established" churches (the term became particularly common in the eighteenth century) – Presbyterian in Scotland, Anglican (or "Episcopalian") in England, Wales, and Ireland. Yet here, the outcome of the seventeenth-century crisis was a concession to religious pluralism that went further than almost anywhere else in Europe. The Parliamentary victory in the Civil Wars, and the beheading of Charles I, with the subsequent, temporary dissolution of the episcopal Church of England, meant that royal absolutism on a continental model was impossible in Britain. After the monarchy was restored under Charles II in 1660, one last attempt was made to harness religious uniformity under the Church of England to political stability. But it failed. The dissenting churches of the years of civil war – churches that were to become the ancestors of the Congregationalist or Independent, English Presbyterian, Baptist, and Quaker churches of familiar name – could not be suppressed. The "bloodless" revolution of 1688, by which the Catholic monarch James II was deposed by a coalition of Anglican churchmen and Dissenters, led inexorably to the granting of more extensive rights to Dissenters, under the Toleration Act of 1689. Now this was still not anything like the modern notion of toleration. The Churches of England and Scotland remained "Established," and supported by a daunting range of legislation designed to protect and enhanced their privileged status. Dissenters, in any case, were relatively thin on the ground.

In the new American colonies, too, the nature of the British settlement by the end of the seventeenth century signaled a corresponding notion of limited toleration. It is extremely difficult to generalize. In many of the colonies, it was practically impossible for an Anglican establishment to come into being with any degree of permanence. In Puritan New England, even at the end of the seventeenth century there was no "official" Establishment of religion, and yet the Independent churches to all intents and purposes were the dominant force in the colonies' religious life. And there were some instances of religious persecution. Indeed, one historian has put it like this: "The reign of the New England Puritan ministers was stern and intolerant. We cannot pretend for a moment that it was otherwise."[5] This was because the founding fathers were determined to try to create in the New World the orderly religious community they believed they had been denied in the Old World. This required the construction of what some have called a theocracy, a society in which religion and civil society were closely entwined. Ministers were powerful local officials. Deviant forms of religion, they believed, could not be tolerated. Quakers were persecuted. Two were even executed on Boston Common in 1658, and others two years later. Quakers were regarded with particular suspicion, partly because of their refusal to take oaths. Yet again America's size and opportunities came to the rescue. William Penn's receipt of what became known as Pennsylvania in 1681 (in payment of a government debt to his father) gave Quakers a colony of their own. No clearer sign could possibly be given of the way in which America's sheer size influenced its history of religious diversity. It also showed, incidentally, how it was impossible, almost from the very beginning, for anything like Europe's established churches to exist in the highly fragmented religious culture of North America.

A religion of restraint

The end of the bitter religious conflicts of seventeenth-century Europe had two consequences worth noting here. The first was that toleration, however limited in practice, did force Christians to begin to accept that other Christians might disagree strongly with them on specific and important matters of faith, but could still command respect. Protestants and Catholics continued to regard each other with suspicion. The charges of "heresy," "schism," and "anti-Christ" were still heard. But they were not used with quite the same intensity as in the preceding era. Mutual acceptance took a long time to arrive. Indeed, it could not be said to have arrived until long into the nineteenth century. Yet religious difference was no longer worth fighting over. That was something.

The second consequence was that, correspondingly, religious conviction lost something of its emotional charge. It became more restrained. By the late seventeenth century, both in Catholicism and in the various forms of Protestantism, on the whole the intensity of the sixteenth and early seventeenth century experience of faith had receded. Later generations, looking back on the religion of the later seventeenth and early eighteenth centuries, were to assume that it had actually lost heart, and become weak and even corrupt. This was not the case. If a certain expression of passion had gone ("enthusiasm" in the eighteenth century was often a term of abuse, implying something close to madness), that did not mean a loss of conviction. The general religious ethos of the period was steady, sober, and confident. This was the age of "rational" religion, by which people – whether they were Catholics or Protestants – meant that Christianity expressed perfectly the constitution of the world at large. Christians might condemn "worldly" temptations, of course, but they had an optimistic assumption that there was no underlying contradiction between a fuller and closer understanding of the world at large, and the practice of Christianity. In Protestantism particularly (though one can see something of the same spirit in Catholicism), there continued to be much interest in the cultivation of the private, inward spiritual life, reflected in the popularity of devotional manuals. In English, one of the most famous was *Holy Living, Holy Dying* (1650–1) by Jeremy Taylor, a seventeenth-century Anglican bishop. Publicly, however, attention was increasingly focused on the sermon. The sermon, not the sacrament, was the high point of the service. Church interiors were often designed around the pulpit or preaching desk, and seats (or high backed "pews") arranged almost like the interior of a theatre. Preachers would expect to use the sermon as a primary vehicle of teaching. They were preoccupied with the theme of duty,

St Paul's Cathedral

conformity to the moral requirements of the faith, and with the evidence of Christianity. They looked to their faith to uphold society, and not to change, disrupt, or overturn it.

All this accorded well with a new concern for order, reflected in changing fashions in art, literature, and architecture. Classicism drew inspiration from the Renaissance, and thus went back even before the Reformation, but its flowering in the arts had been held back by the general impact of civil conflict. Christopher Wren's great successor to the old St Paul's Cathedral in London, destroyed in the "Great Fire" of 1666, was a tribute to classical inspiration. One of the largest cathedrals in western Europe, St Paul's took thirty-five years to build, and was not complete until 1710. Yet it is not difficult to see the stylistic similarities between its design and that of St Peter's in Rome, begun early in the sixteenth century before the Reformation. In fact, it was only in the seventeenth century that the word "Gothic" came into use popularly to describe the medieval style, and at first it was a term of abuse – it meant "barbaric." Classicism, so it was thought, had overcome the barbarism of the "Middle Ages," the time between the admired ancient world and the modern world.

Yet the rise of "rational" religion also reflected a certain self-consciousness on the part of Christians. For the first time in the history of the West, since the Roman Empire, there were now serious intellectual challenges to Christianity emerging. In part, these owed their origin to the striking developments in scientific knowledge underway in post-Reformation Europe. Galileo's cosmology, Harvey's study of the circulation of the blood, and above all Newton's mathematics, and his formulation of what were to be taken for nearly three hundred years as the "laws" of the known universe, could be taken together to suggest that it was perfectly possible to understand the world without recourse to theology. In Britain, at the end of the seventeenth century, for a time a number of thinkers flourished who wanted to strip Christianity of practically all its supernatural features; all that could be shown as true

The Great Fire of London

was the basic belief in a creator God; the rest was mythology, or distortion. It was not difficult to find the flaw in the argument of these "Deists," as they were later called (from the Latin "deus," or "god"): their position was an unstable one, because either you did not need to affirm the existence even of God himself, or the belief in the Christian revelation and all it entailed was every bit as convincing as the basic conviction that God existed. Yet the influence, the skepticism, of these men bore fruit in numerous intellectual circles across Europe and America in the course of the eighteenth century. This was the age of "Enlightenment," when many people thought they were emerging at last from the shadow of "superstition" (a particularly hostile word in the eighteenth century), to use the new knowledge of the natural world as a key to changing society for the better. To varying degrees, they began to reject Christianity, or at least its miraculous claims. Preachers, in turn, reacted often by trying to prove the rational, orderly character of Christianity's miracles. Criticism and faith were bound up together: rational criticism of religion provoked a defense of Christianity as rational.

Where did all this leave the Bible, by the early eighteenth century? For a start, its use had come to reflect the religious division Reformation had opened up in Europe. Catholics and Protestants did not use quite the same Bible. Following the practice of Luther, who in turn drew on an ancient tradition, Protestants had taken out of the Old Testament a number of books that were thought to be of somewhat less authority. These books, which included 1 and 2 Esdras, the Wisdom of Solomon, and 1 and 2 Maccabees, were, for Protestants, printed as "Apocrypha." They remained in the Old Testament used by Catholics, integral as they were to the old Latin Vulgate. But on both sides of the confessional divide, the Bible was now more widely available than ever before. Translated into a host of different languages, through the invention of printing relatively cheap copies could be bought by all but the very poorest. Literacy was still quite limited, but it was generally more extensive than had been the case centuries before. The King James Bible, which had drawn extensively on the earlier, incomplete work of William Tyndale, was published in 1611, but rapidly became established as the authoritative English translation for English-speaking Protestants. Its cadences, and even many of its phrases, like those of Shakespeare and the English *Book of Common Prayer*, were to pass into ordinary usage.

But if the Bible was read more widely than ever before, it was also now beginning to be questioned as never before. In the privileged circles of the intellectual elites of Europe and America, there were now those who doubted the accuracy of the biblical miracles, and who considered the world of the Bible to be much like the mythology of the ancient world. If they did not reject Christianity altogether, many of these early biblical critics were searching for an expression of faith much more in keeping with the ordered, rational view of the world they valued. And even the strictly orthodox could not help imbibing something of the worldly optimism of the Enlightenment thinkers. They lived, so they thought, in a stable, ordered world. They looked back on the wars of religion with horror. They did not want to return to the conflicts provoked by religious "enthusiasm." For all that they owed the Protestant Reformation, if they were Protestants, and the Catholic Reformation, if they were Catholics, they had little desire to re-awaken the fervor of those times. Yet events were to show what a gap this left.

1 H. Bettenson (ed.), *Documents of the Christian Church* (Oxford University Press, London, 1943), p. 156.

2 M. Luther, *To the Christian Nobility of the German Nation*, in *Three Treatises* (Fortress Press, Philadelphia, 1970), p. 22.

3 M. Luther, *The Bondage of the Will* (James Clarke, London, 1957), p. 128.

4 *Tyndale's Old Testament* (ed. By D. Daniell, Yale University Press, New Haven & London, 1992), p. 7.

5 W. L. Sperry, *Religion in America* (Cambridge University Press, 1945).

Chapter 2

A Fresh Spring: the European Origins of the Evangelical Revival

The underbelly of Enlightenment

The story we shall tell of the Evangelical Revival is a story mainly about America and Britain. But the Revival was not, in origin, English-speaking. Its roots lie in German Protestantism. We find there a surprising story of survival and change, in the face of opposition from traditionalist Lutherans as well as Roman Catholics, a story of relatively small communities who nevertheless unlocked a tidal wave of religious feeling that swept across the Protestant churches of the English-speaking world in two or three generations, and changed them forever.

We have seen how the Peace of Westphalia stabilized central Europe after the devastation of the Thirty Years' War. But the Peace, if it tidied up certain aspects of religious division in Europe, still left substantial Protestant minorities in the multitude of states (many of them formally Catholic) in central and southern Germany. These minorities were sometimes actively persecuted. In Silesia, for example, a sizeable Protestant remnant faced determined attempts to suppress their religion, and convert them back to Catholicism. War came to the rescue eventually here – twice, in fact. As part of the Swedish foray into mainland European conflict in what is usually called the "War of the Spanish Succession," in 1707 the Swedish king, Charles XII, marched into Silesia and forced some concessions that favored the Silesian Protestants. Finally, in 1740, Frederick William II of Prussia (Frederick "the Great," as posterity was to label him) annexed the state as a whole to the vigorously expanding, definitely Protestant Prussia. Protestant minorities in Moravia, Bohemia, Salzburg, and even Austria itself were subject to similar pressures. Here, too, the emergence of a powerful north German state, namely Prussia, was also not without its influence. Prussia's expansionism in the late seventeenth and eighteenth centuries, and its policy of encouraging economic development (especially through attracting migrant workers) was a considerable psychological boost to beleaguered Protestants in other states. And not just psychological. Prussia covertly offered material support in many cases, and also sanctuary for those forced to flee under the shadow of war and persecution. In 1731, for example, the Salzburg government finally expelled most of its Protestant population. Though some eventually settled as far afield as the Netherlands, England, and even (as we shall see) America, by far the largest number – over 20,000 – were taken by Prussia, and settled in East Prussia, Pomerania, and even Lithuania.

Frederick the Great

But it would be a mistake to think that all this simply exemplified Protestant solidarity. If Protestants had been forced to act together against a Catholic threat during the seventeenth century, the subsidence of bitter religious conflict had brought their own internal divisions to the fore. Most fundamental of these was that between the Lutherans and the Reformed. Lutheranism was mostly concentrated in northern Europe, Scandinavia, and the Baltic states. Further south, and particularly in Switzerland, as well as in the Netherlands, it was Reformed Protestantism, following the way of Calvin rather than Luther, which was dominant. To the Lutherans, Reformed Protestantism was militant and extreme, and had distorted the true meaning of Scripture. To the Reformed, Lutheranism was a sort of impure Protestantism, a "bastard Protestantism," that had retained too many features of the doctrine and order of the old Church. Lutherans had retained the medieval priesthood, if they had often dispensed with bishops. Lutherans also retained a belief in the real, objective presence of Christ in the consecrated bread and wine of the Eucharist. The Reformed had developed a theology of predestination that went some way beyond Luther's understanding of the freedom of the gospel. This gave Reformed Christianity often a sense of absolute assurance, and concentrated authority, reinforcing the Lutheran perception of it as a militant tendency.

Yet there were many divisions even within these communities. By the seventeenth century, both the Lutheran and Reformed churches had been subject to a process that historians have labeled – awkwardly – "confessionalization." What this means is that the doctrine of the churches had been summarized in confessional documents such as the Augsburg Confession of 1530, which most Lutherans accepted, and then expanded and systematized into rigid orthodoxies, as those churches had become more settled. By the late seventeenth century, this had led to a situation in which the theology of European Protestantism appeared static and formalistic. The tremendous passion and energy of Luther's writing had been dissipated by its submergence into a defensive passivity. At times, "orthodox" Lutheranism, as it was called, could appear trivial, unexciting, and even worldly. The radicalism of the Reformed confessional churches had also declined into pedantry and legalism. Or so it seemed to their critics, at least. In Protestant countries, the clergy constituted a high proportion of the educated, professional classes. Among these people, excitement was generated not by theology, but by the new developments in science, history, and philosophy. Most of these developments were not pioneered by unbelievers. Explicit atheism appeared later, and was never very popular in the Enlightenment. Rather, the early Enlightenment was a development within Christian thought. Yet it stretched and challenged traditional Christian thought in ways that its own proponents could scarcely conceive. In this way, Christianity was the "underbelly' of the Enlightenment. A movement that later generations came to see as critical of religion largely assumed the intrinsic truth of Christianity. And yet its characteristic interests and critical insights took it well beyond traditional Christian theology.

From an array of examples that could include the English mathematician Isaac Newton, let us take instead the German philosopher Gottfried Wilhelm Leibniz (1646–1716). It is for his discovery of the calculus that Leibniz is perhaps best known, though he is also remembered for his formidably difficult essay in metaphysics, the *Monadology* (1720). His conception of the universe as a succession of monads, the highest of which was God, appeared to make God a subject of the world, and not finally the master and maker of it. But Leibniz was born and bred a Lutheran. He published a systematic theology, and appears to have assumed that his extensive literary and philosophical work did not represent a substantial challenge to Christian truth.

Pietism

It was in this context of Protestant "orthodoxy" and intellectual ferment that the source of worldwide revivalism came into being. Pietism, as it has been called, was a reaction against the sterility of the prevailing church culture of northern Germany. It involved the cultivation of an intense, emotional, inward devotion, a conviction of "real religion" in contrast to external formalism. It had – as such movements do – many diverse sources, and many proponents. It drew on elements of genuine Lutheran piety in particular that had survived throughout the turmoil of the mid-seventeenth century, such as the popular devotion associated with the hymns of Paul Gerhardt (1607–76). But its leading figures, for the purposes of our story, were three in number.

The first of these was Philipp Jakob Spener (1635–1705). Brought up in Alsace and Strasburg, he was convinced that the church culture of the German Lutheran churches was moribund. The Church had undergone, in the Reformation, external reform. But it lacked the corresponding internal change. Elements of the old clericalism had remained. In particular, argued Spener, Luther's great insight into the central importance of the priesthood of all believers – the idea that all Christians, however high or low, had the same privileges and authority in principle within the Christian community – had not been allowed to take root properly within the Church. In his *Pia Desideria* (1675), Spener argued for a renewal of the Church along those lines. We can get a flavor of the purpose of the work (and of the reasons why it infuriated Spener's clerical contemporaries) from its sub-title: "*heartfelt desires for an improvement of the true evangelical church pleasing to God, with some Christian proposals to that end.*" Spener's colleagues cannot have liked that word "improvement" much. They had just emerged from years of conflict over religion, and the thought that all that trouble had failed to settle the affairs of the Protestant churches satisfactorily was hardly likely to recommend itself to them. Spener, in the words of one historian, "castigated every class of society for their responsibility for the lamentable state of the Church".[1] The remedy lay in the promotion of small, private meetings for Bible study and mutual spiritual encouragement – cells "for the renewal of the Church."[2] To Spener, Luther's theology of justification through faith alone laid the basis for a real personal transformation in the life of the believer, a "New Birth." The class meetings he founded gave ordinary church people the opportunity to explore and sustain this perception in their own lives. They became little hothouses of religious excitement. They were immensely threatening to the Lutheran authorities in Spener's home state of Saxony.

The politics of central Europe, now, however, became significant. Spener found encouragement from a Prussian government willing to countenance some internal religious reform in the interest of casting itself as the true protector of Protestantism in Europe. Politics and religious reform went hand in hand. In 1691 his moment came. Called to Berlin to act as pastor of St Nicholas's church in 1691, he at last had influence where it mattered. In 1694 he was instrumental in the founding of the University of Halle, where the new movement of piety could find support. It sprouted a huge theological faculty, and rapidly became "the training ground for officials of the expanding Prussian state."[3] Pietism had come of age. It had a vital institutional base in Halle. Though its relationship with church and state authorities was to remain problematic, unlike the later Methodism in England, it was never to pass altogether out of the state churches of northern Germany.

In all this, Spener was aided by August Hermann Francke (1663–1727), one of the first professors at Halle. Francke was not so much an original thinker, as a consummate organizer and systematizer. His contribution to the development of Pietism was doctrinal and practical. In doctrine, he took Spener's original insight into a devotional life of the spirit, and its roots in Luther's theology of justification, and turned it into a systematic presentation of the stages of the Christian life. Now the characteristic "Evangelical" pattern emerged of personal conviction of sin under the law, fear of judgment, rejection of a disordered, sinful life, conversion, and then sanctification through continual cultivation of the spiritual life. This pattern was so characteristic and neat that it could be turned into an easily learned, easily transmitted way of describing Christian discipleship. Spener and Francke between them had shaped a way of understanding the religious life of the individual that was to travel very far. It could be translated with ease into a different linguistic and church context. Its concentration on the religious life of the individual made it peculiarly attractive within Protestant circles. It was a development of existing insights and convictions within Protestantism, and so it touched familiar elements of church life throughout the Protestant world. And yet it had a new, characteristic spirit of its own. Nor was it exclusively the preserve of the individual. It could reach and transform church life as a whole. In practical terms, Francke massively enhanced Spener's vision of a renewed church life. He demonstrated at Halle, alongside the new university, that Pietism could promote organized social welfare on a scale unheard of before. He founded an orphanage that, with over 3,000 inmates and workers, became one of the largest buildings in Europe, and a dispensary ("the first producer of standardized branded medicaments on a commercial scale"), a printing press, a Bible Institute, schools, and a teacher's training institution.[4] This was Pietism as a whole social experiment. Society could be convicted of sin, converted, and transformed just like the individual. Moreover, Francke's idea of social transformation was for export. From the printing presses of Halle, Bibles and religious literature, often translated into the myriad languages of Eastern Europe, poured out across Europe.

Had Francke's vision been allied to decisive government support from other states, it might have spread far outside Prussia. But that was not to be. By the middle

The philosopher and mathematician Gottfried Wilhelm Leibnitz was born and brought up as a Lutheran

of the eighteenth century, Prussia under Frederick William II was the dominant power in northern Germany, and yet it was also constantly fighting for its life. Other states were not so enamored of organized Pietism. And even in Prussia church and government officials remained somewhat suspicious of this new way of doing things. Pietism was a controversial development within Lutheranism in particular, a sort of hybrid that was to outgrow its original context. It was Count Nicholas von Zinzendorf (1700–60), a German nobleman, who was most instrumental in its transplantation. Zinzendorf was a deeply pious and emotional man, whose Christian faith, nurtured in the Pietism of Spener and Francke, took the form of an almost simplistic trust in Jesus, the Lamb of God. A landowner, he offered sanctuary to persecuted Protestants from neighboring states. In 1722, Moravian refugees fleeing persecution by the Habsburgs were encouraged to settle on his estates at Herrnhut. Here he formed them into a closely-knit community, whose strong, Christ-centered faith was supplemented by community discipline. In 1727, this community experienced its first "revival," in a form that was to become characteristic. Prayer over several days and nights built up to an afternoon service on 10 August, in which the local pastor was so overcome by his sense of the nearness of God that he threw himself on the ground. Three days later, on 13 August, during a communion service, the assembled congregation experienced what Zinzendorf regarded as an outpouring of the Holy Spirit. This led to a commitment to hourly prayer by some members of the community. In time, the "Moravian Brethren" were to evolve into a new denomination, the "renewed Church of the Brethren," or more simply, the Moravian Church. But not before their influence had touched Protestants more widely.

A Protestant world

At the beginning of the eighteenth century, communications across Europe and between Europe and America remained slow and difficult. A message written in London could take weeks to reach its destination in the colonies. Roads were poor, often no more than dust tracks that turned into a quagmire of mud in heavy rain and in winter. Only the wealthy could afford decent carriages. Horses were expensive to keep. The poor had to walk, or beg a lift from passing agricultural wagons. Travel was dangerous, too. Law enforcement was difficult even in long-settled parts of Europe, and robbers and highwaymen were a hazard to rich and poor alike. Inland in America, there was always the threat of hostile Native Americans. Yet, in the face of conditions such as this, news traveled, and people were on the move, to an almost unprecedented extent. Throughout the late seventeenth and eighteenth centuries, the rise of British sea power, the growth of English-speaking colonies in North America, and the close links between Britain and the Protestant powers of northern Europe helped to forge for a time a chain of Protestant havens, and a Protestant seaboard. When Pietism began to outgrow Germany, there were places where it could go. Protestantism had become an international currency of ideas, now almost rivaling the geographical reach of Catholicism. The displacement of Protestant communities in central Europe spilled over into other states.

Some of the persecuted Moravian Protestants came to Britain. They settled mostly in London, which had long acted as a safe haven for exiled Lutheran and Reformed communities. There were Dutch, German Lutheran, and Swiss Reformed churches in London. As early as 1550 the nave of an abandoned Augustinian friary near what is now the Bank of England had been given to Protestant refugees from the Netherlands for their use. Further west, outside the old city walls, the Savoy Chapel, once part of the Hospital of St John of the Savoy, was used by French-speaking Reformed Protestants. The dissenting sects created during the civil war and commonwealth period in the middle of the seventeenth century all had congregations in London. The arrival of yet another variation on the Protestant theme barely raised an eyebrow.

Across the ocean, too, German refugees settled. The Salzburger Protestants expelled in 1731 had already been influenced by Pietism. Most, as we have seen, settled in Prussia, but a contingent of some 200 were subsidized by Britain and settled at Savannah in Georgia, where John and Charles Wesley were, for a time, to have some religious responsibility for them. Moravian emigrants found their way to the colonies throughout the 1730s, settling particularly in Savannah, Georgia, and then later in Bethlehem, Pennsylvania.

By then, Pietism was crossing church and language boundaries. It was spreading to the English-speaking churches in particular. It was no coincidence that it took root in the Church of England, an "Established" church with strong government support and a position of legal privilege, just as it had originated within the "Established" churches of northern and central Europe. Its leading proponents in Europe all shared the common European assumption that it was the duty of government to uphold and support religious truth. That meant promoting a particular church. Spener, Francke, and even Zinzendorf were, like the Wesleys, convinced, however, that these "official" churches were in danger of settling into neglect and spiritual torpor. They needed revival. Yet this conviction was to lead, almost inevitably, to conflict with church authorities in Britain, as in Germany. It was a different story in America. Here, the sheer variety of colonial settlement made it impossible to impose one version of Christianity on the colonists. In certain areas, such as New England, particular traditions were indeed dominant. But the size and opportunities of America ruled out the creation of religious monopolies. It was here that the immense, expansive energy of revivalism was to find its true home.

1 W. R. Ward, *Faith and Faction* (Epworth, London, 1993), p. 177.

2 *Ibid., loc. cit.*

3 G. R. Cragg, *The Church in the Age of Reason 1648–1789* (Pelican, London, 1960), p. 102.

4 Ward, *Faith and Faction*, p. 79.

Chapter 3

NEW FRONTIERS OF THE HEART: AMERICA AND BRITAIN

The frontier

Pietism traveled far. It became the seed that germinated in the religious soil of America and Britain. But why did it become so influential there, when its position was always under threat in central and northern Europe? To put the question this way is a little misleading. It would certainly not be true to suggest that the Great Awakening, as it is called in America, or the Evangelical Revival, as it is called in Britain, was simply a German export adapted to English-speaking conditions. Pietism provided the inspiration and model for the great American and British exponents of Protestant revival in the eighteenth century, but it was never more than one element of revival. To its systematization of conviction of sin and of conversion, and its appeal to the emotions and to the importance of small groups, we must add many of the characteristic elements of Anglo-Saxon Christianity. The emphasis on the Bible was one of these – an emphasis shared to some extent by the Pietists, but present already within Anglo-Saxon Protestantism. Another was the desire to reshape popular morality and culture along more rigorous lines. That was the spirit of Puritan England and Puritan New England, and it resurfaced in the various Societies for the Reformation of Manners founded in England in the 1690s. Another important element was deliberate missionary activity, sponsored already in the early eighteenth century through the foundation in England of the Society for the Propagation of Christian Knowledge in 1698, which aimed to supply missionaries to the colonies and to found parochial libraries, and the Society for the Propagation of the Gospel in 1701. It was not only German Protestants who wished to reinvigorate the Church.

But the question is nevertheless still pertinent. There was something characteristic about the British and American situations that made them particularly susceptible to religious revival. Both, for quite different reasons, presented the possibility of an expanding frontier of religious activity. In America this was, quite simply, a geographical frontier. The almost ceaseless expansion of the American colonies in the eighteenth century, and then of the states in the early nineteenth century, gave unlimited opportunities for religious growth. It also made American religious life remarkably unsettled. Whereas Britain and Ireland were covered in a network of ancient parishes that had been in existence for almost a thousand years, each served by a local parish church, in America everything had to start from scratch. The eastern seaboard was, as we have seen, settled at different times by different communities of religious belief. The Church of England, the "official" church of the colonizing power, was never very numerous in America, but what strength it had was concentrated in these eastern settlements. Its position was rapidly outflanked by the growth of other Protestant traditions further west.

Moreover, in America this expanding physical frontier was linked to an internal factor, the possibility of constant religious development and change. For the religious pluralism of America, put together with its geographical expansion, made government control of religious development impossible. There was, in other words, an internal frontier, the nature of which could only be discovered by testing in each and every place what kind of religious expression people were prepared to countenance. Except for a short time in the few colonies in which particular religious traditions were powerful, in the long run there was nothing to stop people breaking away from one church and founding another. But the new religious currents of feeling about to burst in the Great Awakening were remarkably adaptable. They could be expressed in traditional churches. They could transform from within existing dissenting traditions, such as the Congregationalists and Baptists. They could sponsor or promote new forms of religious belonging altogether, such as Methodism. Their flexibility derived from their relative indifference to what are called questions of church order – namely the actual form of organizations and hierarchies that run churches – combined with a coherent set of common principles.

But even in Britain and Ireland it makes some sense to speak of an expanding internal frontier. There, too, the population was rising throughout the eighteenth and nineteenth centuries, from perhaps around a total of 7 million in 1700 to over 16 million by 1801, the date of the first official census of Britain and Ireland. In time, by the end of the eighteenth century, it was clear that the distribution of population growth was not even, but concentrated in the rapidly expanding industrial towns and cities. The established churches of Britain could not readily adjust. Their very connection with government inhibited rapid growth. Furthermore, internal difficulties often weakened their ministry. As a result, even in the face of official disapproval, there proved to be plenty of scope for minority, dissenting traditions to survive, and for the new currents of religious feeling to find expression within the established churches themselves.

The Great Awakening

The hunger of people in the new, expanding colonies of America for spiritual transformation and growth was signaled in early outbreaks of religious enthusiasm in the late seventeenth century. Solomon Stoddard (1643–1729) was minister in Northampton, Massachusetts for nearly sixty years. He matched a concern for church discipline with a desire to renew the faith of the "lost," and deliberately sought to make conversions by preaching against the falling-away of the children of

Jonathan Edwards

the faithful. But it was not until the late 1720s that revivalism truly got under way. It was the coming together of innumerable influences and movements that made up the "Great Awakening," usually confined by historians to the two decades from 1730, but for our purposes a broader current running into the second half of the eighteenth century. There were already concentrated bursts of intense evangelistic activity in various places. In Northampton, Massachusetts, Jonathan Edwards was already stirring his congregation with powerful preaching, dwelling on their spiritual danger if inattentive to Christ's commands. In New Jersey, Theodore Frelinghuysen (1691–1747), infused with Pietist ideals from his native Netherlands, had also begun to preach widely and raise a following. Others active in this way included the Presbyterian Gilbert Tennent (1703–64) in Pennsylvania. Tennent was born in northern Ireland, and influenced by Frelinghuysen. His impassioned, revivalist preaching helped to stir up congregations in the middle colonies, and in Pennsylvania in particular.

But it was the agency of George Whitefield (1714–70) that was decisive. Whitefield was a Church of England deacon, whom we shall encounter again shortly when we turn to look at Great Britain. Born in Gloucester and from a humble background, he came under the influence of the Wesley brothers in Oxford, and followed them to Georgia in 1738. But he soon emerged from their shadow. A man of stern but passionate nature, Whitefield was an immensely energetic preacher, who traveled widely in America, gathering out-of-doors congregations of thousands whom

George Whitefield

Prayer meeting outside a Settler log cabin

he convinced of their sin and provoked toward penitence and conversion. He made seven trips in all to America, raising money for the orphanage he had founded in Georgia (the influence of August Francke's Halle experiment is evident here). Almost from the beginning, the effect of his preaching was sensational. He knew how to stir emotion, and preached forcefully and directly, without notes. It is hardly surprising that his early inclination, before his conversion, had been to become an actor. His voice and delivery were so dramatic that Benjamin Franklin was later to claim that even the way he pronounced the word "Mesopotamia" could reduce people to tears. His second trip to the colonies, in 1739 to 1740, galvanized the growing forces of revival. During 1740, he traveled virtually the entire length of the colonies, from Charleston and Savannah in the south, to Philadelphia and New York in the north, and on to New England. During the autumn of 1740, in New England alone, he preached to crowds of over 8,000 almost every day.

The simplicity and passion of Whitefield's message is evident still today in the sermons that have survived in published form. Here he is, for example, on the gift of the Holy Spirit in conversion:

> Be humble therefore, O believers, be humble: look to the rock from whence you have been hewn: extol free grace; admire electing love, which alone has made you to differ from the rest of your brethren. Has God brought you into light? Walk as becometh children of light. Provoke not the Holy Spirit to depart from you: for though he hath sealed you to the day of redemption, and you know that the Prince of

> this world is judged; yet if you backslide, grow luke-warm, or forget your first love, the Lord will visit your offenses with the rod of affliction, and your sin with spiritual scourges. Be not therefore high-minded, but fear. Rejoice, but let it be with trembling. As the elect of God, put on, not only humbleness of mind, but bowels of compassion; and pray, O pray for your unconverted brethren![1]

But to measure the effectiveness of his preaching, we have to turn to surviving eye-witness accounts, often published in diaries and autobiographies. One example is that of Nathan Cole, a farmer from Kensington in Connecticut, who heard Whitefield in 1740. The encounter changed his life. As he recounted it,

> When I saw Mr Whitfield . . . he Lookt almost angelical; a young, Slim, slender, youth before some thousands of people with a bold undaunted Countenance, and my hearing how God was with him every where as he came along it Solemnized my mind; and put me into a trembling fear before he began to preach; for he looked as if he was Clothed with authority from the Great God; and a sweet sollome solemnity sat upon his brow And my hearing him preach, gave me heart wound; By Gods blessing: my old Foundation was broken up, and I saw that my righteousness would not save me; then I was convinced of the doctrine of Election.[2]

The reference here, and in the extract from Whitefield's sermon, to "election" needs some explanation. Whitefield followed a broadly Calvinist view of God's judgment and salvation. He believed, that is, that God, out of his providence, long before the creation of the world had foreordained the entire course his creation would take. That included the "election" of the just, those who would be saved, and the damnation of the unjust. So the judgment God would pass on human beings had already been determined. But it did not follow that human beings should simply acquiesce, passively, in whatever life threw at them, secure either in the knowledge of their salvation, or resigned to their damnation. Far from it. Human beings could not know what God had intended for them. And in a sense, their response to God's call to penitence and conversion, if sincere, could be said to have been included in God's foreordination, since God foresaw everything. The urgency of conversion was thus intensified by God's election, in Whitefield's view.

This "Calvinist" view was common enough in Whitefield's day. It was shared by many of his contemporaries. And it found a ready reception in the American congregations descended from dissenting churches in Britain, and even in many Anglican congregations. Through his amazing energy, revival swept through the colonial churches. But others, too, had their role to play. The most famous of these was Jonathan Edwards (1703–58). Edwards was the grandson of Solomon Stoddard, minister of Northampton, Massachusetts, whose role as a precursor of the Great Awakening we have already noted. Edwards assisted his grandfather and then succeeded to his position when Stoddard died in 1729. Before Whitefield began his preaching tours of America, Edwards began to urge spiritual renewal on his own congregation, with success. Indeed, his *Faithful Narrative of the Surprizing Work of God in Northampton in New England* (1737) had a significant impact on one John Wesley, who read it in England in 1738. A powerful preacher himself, Edwards is best known today as America's foremost theologian, perhaps the greatest exponent of revivalist theology in American history. His best-known sermon is "Sinners in the Hands of an Angry God," delivered in Enfield, Connecticut on 8 July 1741. It is a systematic exploration of the idea of God's providence, God's sustaining hand, taking as its starting-point the apparently simple text from the Book of Deuteronomy, "Their foot shall slide in due time" (Deut. 32:35). Edwards characteristically described the terrors of hell in alluring terms. But he was particularly alert to the dangers of the religiously complacent, those who assumed they were saved because they observed the surface requirements of religion, but who had not been truly transformed by God's grace in their inner being:

> The use of this awful subject may be for awakening unconverted persons in this congregation. This that you have heard is the case of every one of you that are out of Christ. – That world of misery, that lake of burning brimstone, is extended abroad under you. There is the dreadful pit of the glowing flames of the wrath of God ... there is nothing between you and hell but the air; it is only the power and pleasure of God that holds you up. You probably are not sensible of this; you find that you are kept out of hell, but do not see the hand of God in it; but look at other things, at the good state of your bodily constitution, your care of your own life, and the means you use for your preservation. But indeed these things are nothing; if God should withdraw his hand, they would avail no more to keep you from falling, than the thin air to hold up a person that is suspended in it.[3]

Edwards's preaching was certainly of great effect, galvanizing many of those who heard him into a re-examination of their faith and their lives. His fame as a preacher of revival spread far and wide, though it was never as great in his lifetime as that of Whitefield. But it is as a theologian above all that he is remembered today. In a series of works that became immensely influential in America, he developed his exposition of the theory of religious revival into a much more searching exploration of God's saving of his elect. In A *Treatise concerning Religious Affections* (1746), he warned his fellow Americans of the danger of excessive reliance on emotional stimulation: true faith was seen, not in the intensity of feeling, but in changing of a person's heart so that they sought above all else the love of God. In *Freedom of the*

Will (1754), and *Original Sin* (1758), perhaps Edwards's two greatest works, he demonstrated how all-embracing was the nature of human sin, and how illusory was human freedom. True conversion required an infusion of God's grace to transform the sinful heart and turn its motives toward desire for God. Finally, in *The Nature of True Virtue* (1765), published after his death, Edwards distinguished between mere worldly goodness, and the true morality founded on God's grace. In all his works, true to his Calvinist roots, Edwards's abiding theme was the overpowering majesty and grandeur of God, and the paucity of human resources for moral improvement without an experience of God's grace.

Even Edwards, for all the impact and power of his preaching, was not above controversy, however. The revivals stimulated by his, by Whitefield's, and by others' work revitalized the faith of many thousands of people. But they also created tensions within existing communities of Christians. They appeared to value the experience of those who claimed dramatic conversion experiences above that of those who followed the way of faith quietly and humbly. They could lead to superficial comparison between "real Christians" and the unregenerate. It was this that Edwards had argued against in A *Treatise concerning Religious Affections*. Yet in Edwards's own congregation, objections were raised to his practice, late in his years as a minister, of restricting communion only to those members of his congregation who were "professedly regenerate," and he was forced out of his position. He retired to a small charge at Stockbridge, Massachusetts, finding more time to concentrate on his theological writing.

In America, as was also to be the case in Britain, the very techniques deployed by revivalist preachers such as Edwards and Whitefield were often at the same time the trigger for hostility. They encouraged the formation of the newly converted into small groups or classes, which met to support each other, to pray together, and to study the Bible together. In this way, once again like the Pietists of central and northern Germany, they found a way to renew the commitment of

Protestant Christianity to the regular reading of the Bible. Yet small groups were often threatening to those who felt they were left on the outside, and also to established ministers who were not part of the revival movement. These tensions were often increased by the development of lay and itinerant ministry, with ordinary people being charged to lead Bible classes, or to tour the countryside and towns, often raising a crowd in the open air and preaching the Word of God. Sometimes these lay preachers were women – in itself a matter of controversy. The theology of revival depended, too, on emphasizing the laxity and deficiency of the Christianity of existing congregations – not a message many ministers wanted to hear. So revival brought conflict in its wake, and stirred up passions that frequently found their outlet in the division of congregations, and the founding of new congregations and even of new Christian denominations altogether. In this way, the effect of the Great Awakening was not only to rejuvenate the life of the existing churches, but to give encouragement to those who passed outside the existing churches, and in the process to transform the overall shape of American Christianity.

By the 1750s, when the first great surge of interest sparked by the Great Awakening was beginning to die down, its effects could be seen in different ways in different parts of the colonies. In New England, for example, the dominance of the older Puritan churches was broken, and there were now four main groups of churches. Some, under the influences of revival, were encouraged to break away from the Puritan churches altogether. Called "libertarians" by some, they rejected any church–state link at all, and many became Baptist. Another group of churches remained within the Congregationalist fold, but were evidently transformed by the revival. These were called the "New Lights," and they included for example Jonathan Edwards's congregation at Northampton. These "hoped to maintain the traditional ties between church and state," but definitely subordinated this to the renewal of the faith of church members.[4] The "Old Calvinists" were the third group, who remained faithful to the older Puritan way and were somewhat resistant to the effects of the new revivalism. Finally, some Congregationalists, joined by some Anglicans, reacted against revivalism so that they were drawn toward Enlightenment rationalism, and ultimately Unitarianism (the denial that Jesus Christ was divine). In the middle colonies, faced already with religious diversity of a kind that did not exist in New England, the impact of the Great Awakening was to transform the spiritual life of all the denominations, and to lead to the formation of something like a common Evangelical culture in the long run. In the southern colonies, the revivals broke the local influence of Anglicanism for good, and led to the rise of the Baptist churches, which provided an emotional, personal form of religion in contrast to the formal ceremonialism of Anglican worship.

Britain: the rise of Methodism

Just as there were key personalities in the Great Awakening in America, especially Whitefield and Edwards, on whom historians have tended to light, so too the history of revivalism in Britain is impossible to describe without giving significant space to the brothers John and Charles Wesley, and also to Whitefield again. Yet here too, in practice the situation was much more complex. Revival would have come to Britain in some form without the Wesleys. It would perhaps have been weaker, and less well organized, and might not eventually have led to the formation of a new Christian church altogether, the Methodist church, but it would have happened.

The evidence for this is what happened in Wales. Revival came to Wales long before it came to England. Griffith Jones (1683–1761), Rector of Llandowror in south Wales, "preached an evangelical Calvinism" from early in his ministry. In 1714 he sparked off a small revival in the towns and villages around Llandowror, anticipating the greater revival of the 1730s.[5] Jones in fact got into trouble with his bishop, because he preached in the open air, and did not confine himself to his church. Jones's action, reminiscent of the unregulated preaching of the religious chaos of the mid-seventeenth century in Britain, was copied by the great Howell

Harris (1714–73), who was not ordained, but became an itinerant preacher nonetheless, traveling the length and breadth of Wales and in northern England. Harris and his friend Daniel Rowlands (1713–90) began their traveling in 1736, Harris claiming indeed that he was "the first itinerant preacher of Redemption in this period of the Revival."[6] The early outbreak of revival in Wales was to foreshadow the great Evangelical culture of Wales in the nineteenth and early twentieth centuries.

But it is to the Wesleys we must turn now, for their impact on revival in England was decisive. John Wesley (1703–91) and Charles Wesley (1707–88) were sons of an Anglican clergyman, born in the rectory at Epworth in South Yorkshire that still stands as a museum to the brothers. John was almost burned to death as a child when the old rectory caught fire, and in adult life was fond of describing himself as a "brand plucked from the burning." This sense of being marked out for a special work was to stay with him all his life. As a Fellow at Oxford, he joined a small group of devout students, the "Holy Club," who included his brother Charles, and the young George Whitefield. It was here, as a jibe against the members of the club, that the name "Methodist" was coined, meaning that the members of the club were too "methodical" in their approach to religion. Under the direction of the SPCK, the brothers went out to Georgia in America in 1735 to carry out missionary duties, but this trip failed, partly due to John's atrocious, inexperienced preaching, and partly to his disastrous courtship of a local girl, and they returned home ignominiously two years later. Now the Moravian link came into play. The small community of Moravian Protestants in London included one Peter Boehler, who befriended the Wesleys. Throughout the early months of 1738, John was in frequent contact with Boehler, discussing matters of faith. Boehler urged on John the necessity of a real, inner conversion, adding pressure to John's own evident sense that he lacked inner conviction: "Preach faith till you have it," advised Boehler, "and then because you have it, you will preach faith."[7] It was at the Moravians' meeting at a house in

Aldersgate Street on 24 May 1738 that Wesley had his famous "heart-warming" experience. As he described it in his journal:

> In the evening I went very unwillingly to a society in Aldersgate Street, where one was reading Luther's preface to the Epistle to the Romans. About a quarter before nine, while he was describing the change which God works in the heart through faith in Christ, I felt my heart strangely warmed. I felt I did trust in Christ, Christ alone, for salvation; and an assurance was given me that He had taken away my sins, even mine, and saved me from the law of sin and death.[8]

This is one of the most famous conversion accounts of all time. But it is important to bear in mind that Wesley had long been a convinced Christian, indeed a clergyman and an evangelical Christian, before this. This experience was like a special assurance of God's grace, which confirmed him in the course on which he was already set. Shortly after this, John traveled to Marienbon to meet Count von Zinzendorf, and then on to Herrnhut. There he saw at first hand the practical organization and life of the Moravians. Their members were organized into classes and "bands," a system he and Charles had already copied in Georgia. Their services of agape ("love feast") and vigilae ("watch night" services) were to be copied into Methodism. So too was their practice of frequent hymn-singing. This was of incalculable importance for the Evangelical revival, for hymns could be learnt easily by an illiterate or poor congregation, and their catchy tunes could be the means of learning the doctrine and sentiments carefully embedded in their words.

Returning to England, in 1739 Wesley's ministry outside Oxford and London began to take off. Encouraged by George Whitefield, who had begun preaching to large crowds outside Bristol, Wesley took over the leadership and organization of these Bristol followers. Gradually his ministry widened still further. Traveling always by horse, which he rode with a "slack rein," so that he could read as he rode, he covered hundreds of thousands of miles in the next fifty years. The popular image of Wesley as a village preacher is a little misleading, however. He disliked preaching in the rural areas, convinced he could do little good there, and concentrated on the poor and the "middling sort" of the towns and cities, particularly the growing industrial towns. It was his supporters, the few clergy who followed him, and the new itinerant lay preachers, who spread the word in the parishes up and down the country. As they preached, new groups of followers were called together by the intense experience of receiving the message of salvation, conviction of their sin, and the assurance that they were saved. These new followers, following the Moravian pattern, were organized into "societies" in each place, and into smaller "classes" for regular meetings. At the center of it all was Wesley himself, a warm, generous, but always strict and controlling authority. In later life, perhaps out of affection, perhaps in jest, he was nicknamed "Pope John."

Just what, exactly, made Methodism so attractive to the laboring poor? Much ink has been spilled trying to answer that question. Like the revivalism Whitefield, Edwards and others were promoting across the ocean, Methodism offered an intense, practical experience of conversion and renewal. The vast majority of those who responded would have been baptized in their local parish church, some of them would perhaps have attended their parish church from time to time (or more regularly), and all would have considered themselves "Christian." But the religion of the established Church did not offer them an emotional commitment of the kind that followed conversion according to Wesley's preaching. Moreover, Wesley's emphasis was very much on the assurance of God's forgiveness, and on the real progress that the transformed believer could make toward perfection. At the center of his "system" or "method" lay the study of the Bible. Through the classes, the Bible could be read and endlessly discussed by the poor themselves. Some would claim that Wesley was merely fulfilling the Reformation promise to bring the Bible into the homes of the poor. In fact many had possessed the Bible for a long time, and read it in their own time. And yet it is true that, through the classes, Wesley had found a means – other than that of preaching in the churches – to open up its message more widely to the poor. More than almost anyone else in the history of Christianity in the West, Wesley, like the great American revivalists we have met already, made it possible for Christians to be a people of the Book.

Yet the rise of Methodism was not without controversy. Eventually one source of opposition to the Wesley brothers and their work was the followers of Whitefield himself. Whitefield always remained a friend and supporter of John Wesley. But there was a gap between their views. The gap at first seemed narrow, but it widened into a gulf. Whitefield, as we have seen, was Calvinist in his theology. The call was to the many to examine their consciences, but it was always in the knowledge that the few were chosen. God's judgment was already issued, in the mists of time. Wesley, by contrast, was Arminian in his theology – that is, he believed that the call was genuinely still open to all. In Charles' and John's hymns, this sense that Jesus' death and resurrection encompassed all in its saving work was expressed very powerfully:

> The world he suffered to redeem
> For all he hath the atonement made
> For those that will not come to him
> The ransom of his life was paid.[9]

Whitefield and his followers were unhappy at the apparently indiscriminate nature of this Arminian view, thinking it cheapened God's grace. Whitefield, who never had quite the impact in England that he had in America, continued to address large crowds, and gathered his followers into a group of congregations patronized and financially supported by the Countess of Huntingdon. Selina Shirley (1707–91) had married the 9th Earl of Huntingdon, and after his death devoted much of her fortune to the founding of chapels (some 64 in all), and the creation of a theological college for Calvinist preachers at Trevecca in Wales. The "Countess of Huntingdon's Connexion'", as it was called, in effect eventually separated from the Wesleys, and also from the Church of England. After Whitefield's death in 1770, many of his followers, unchecked now, turned on Wesley, criticizing and lampooning him. For a time, this breach between Arminianism and Calvinism was a serious division in English Evangelicalism.

The other source of opposition was the established Church itself. In the first ten years or so of Wesley's traveling ministry, he encountered bitter opposition from local people, stirred up often by the clergy and the gentry. Sometimes he even met with mob violence. In 1744–5, the rioting against Wesley was particularly ferocious in Cornwall, and in Staffordshire. But this form of opposition gradually died down. The hostility of many of the clergy, and certainly of most of the bishops, did not. Wesley himself, and his brother, never desired to create a new church outside the Church of England. To the very end of his life, Wesley considered himself a loyal member of the Church of England. But his Methodist revivalism cut across the settled, parish ministry of the established Church. Local clergy were resentful. They thought Methodism was schismatic, and that it encouraged delusions of spiritual insight and pride. The itinerant, lay preachers looked to be undermining the legal authority of the Church of England. Eventually, near his death,

Selina, Countess of Huntingdon

Wesley was forced to recognize the inevitable. His new movement could not be accommodated within the Church of England. To serve the "Wesleyan" Methodists established in America cut adrift from England after the American Revolution, he had already broken his own church's rules and ordained new ministers. Now the system had to be extended to England. With his death, in 1791, the new Wesleyan Methodist Church had come into being.

What, in the end, had the Wesleys accomplished? They had, for one thing, created a new church, an Evangelical church called the Methodist Connexion (they used the word "connexion," rather than "church" to describe the network of local Methodist societies). When Wesley died in 1791, the surge in members later in his life meant that membership had risen to over 72,000.[10] This figure denotes only full, adult, committed members, and does not include children and "hangers on." So the actual numbers falling within the Methodist sphere of influence would have been much larger than that. This was a serious challenge to the established Church of England, and yet its threat was somewhat mitigated by the fact that, for decades to come, many Methodists remained supportive of their local parish churches, and even continued to attend them once on Sundays. The Methodist societies were the most obvious result of Evangelical revival in England. The Wesleys had, of course, traveled further afield, to Wales, Ireland, and even to Scotland. But revival had come to Wales anyway, and it was also coming to churches both inside and outside England that remained officially untouched by the Wesleys. And even the established churches – the Anglican churches of England, Ireland, and Wales, and the Presbyterian Church of Scotland – were themselves beginning to develop their own Evangelical revivalist movements. The Wesleys certainly had some, perhaps unintended, influence on all of this. From the Moravian influence, they had developed a model of organization that some revivalists were to copy or adapt. They had also developed a theological emphasis on assurance and Christian perfection that was to be copied by some, and criticized by others. They had developed a practice of hymn-singing, and the emotional language of real encounter with Jesus Christ to go with it, that was to be even more influential still. Methodism was to remain a distinct and permanent force within Evangelical Protestantism. But its importance went beyond that. It had become the spearhead of revival in Britain.

1 George Whitefield, 'The Holy Spirit Convincing the World of Sin, Righteousness and Judgment', *in Selected Sermons of George Whitefield*, http://www.ccel.org/ccel/whitefield/sermons.all.html#xli.

2 Quoted in Mark Noll, *A History of Christianity in the United States and Canada* (SPCK, London, 1992), p. 93.

3 J. Edwards, 'Sinners in the Hands of an Angry God', http://www.ccel.org/e/edwards/sermons/sinners.html, p. 1.

4 Noll, op. cit., p. 98.

5 J. D. Walsh, 'The Origins of the Evangelical Revival', in G. V. Bennett & J. D. Walsh, *Essays in Modern Church History* (A & C Black, London, 1966), p. 134.

6 A Brief Account of the Life of Howell Harris (1791), quoted in J. D. Walsh, op. cit., p. 135.

7 Quoted in M. Edwards, 'John Wesley', in R. Davies & G. Rupp (eds), *A History of the Methodist Church in Great Britain*, Vol. 1 (Epworth Press, London, 1965), pp. 48-9.

8 J. Wesley, Journal, at http://www.ccel.org/w/wesley/journal/journal.htm.

9 From Charles Wesley, Hymns on God's Everlasting Love (1741), quoted in G. Wakefield, 'John and Charles Wesley: A Tale of Two Brothers', in G. Rowell (ed.), *The English Religious Tradition and the Genius of Anglicanism* (Ikon, Wantage, 1992), p. 180.

10 J. D. Walsh, 'Methodism at the end of the eighteenth century', in Davies & Rupp, op. cit., p. 278.

Chapter 4

EVANGELICALISM TRIUMPHANT

THE RESULTS OF the Great Awakening in America and of the Methodist revival in Britain were spectacular enough in the mid-eighteenth century, but they were limited in their way. They did not directly affect the majority of Protestants in either country at first. For every one whose faith was transformed by the experience of converting grace, and the assurance of salvation, there were many others who soldiered on in the ways they had always followed, faithful to their church tradition and suspicious of this new emotionalism and enthusiasm. Yet, by the end of the century, it became clear that something much more profound was under way in Protestantism in Britain and America. As we have seen, the effects of revivalism began to spread more widely. The growth of evangelicalism continued apace, and by the middle of the nineteenth century, it had come to dominate church life in all of the main Protestant denominations on both sides of the Atlantic. From a lively, vigorous but controversial minority, it had come to embrace the experience of much of the Protestant world. It was indeed triumphant.

As it spread, it transformed existing denominations, and triggered the formation of new denominations. Schism was often a sign of vitality. People argued over things they cared about. Had God already determined the fate of the majority of people, or was it possible to change the outcome of divine judgment? What authority did the clergy have? Should church members be expelled for backsliding, or forgiven and permitted to continue their church association? Was communion important in the Christian community or not? Would Jesus come again soon and usher in a reign of a thousand years before the end of the world, or was his coming itself to signal the end of the world, and begin a reign of a kind literally inconceivable to any human mind? How closely should one observe the Sabbath? Should one abstain from all alcoholic drinks (even communion wine), or was some drinking in moderation permissible? These questions, and others like them, perplexed our forebears not because their minds were full of trivial matters, but because religion was so important to them that differences of belief assumed enormous significance in practical terms. And if others disagreed strongly with you, and forced you out of the church, what was to stop you, and your friends, founding another church and appointing your own minister?

Even so, for all the disagreements between different groups of Protestants, something like a common Evangelical culture was coming into being. It had common spiritual resources, for one thing. Chief among these was, of course, the Bible, almost always in the English-speaking world in the "King James" version of 1611. Evangelicals followed the Reformation principle of the authority of Holy Scripture alone, *sola scriptura*. At first, this was not particularly contentious. They definitely regarded the Church's traditions as of limited authority, but generally speaking all Protestants shared a similar sense of the priority of Scripture. Difficulties came later, in the early to mid-nineteenth century, when Christianity was faced with the challenges to the authority of the Bible coming from new discoveries in science, and the growth of historical analysis of the Bible. Then, Protestants were forced to choose between different approaches to interpreting the Bible. But the Bible was always central to Evangelical religion. Households would have their own family

John Milton dictating Paradise Lost

Bibles, often inscribing the births, marriages, and deaths of family members in the endpapers. Literate households, under the influence of Evangelicalism, by the early nineteenth century might have a daily reading of Scripture aloud, as well as a concentrated period of biblical study on Sundays. The Bible was a guide to daily life, a gift of heaven, and a comfort in suffering.

But there were other spiritual resources, too. They included certain "classics" of Christian writing, such as the medieval Thomas a Kempis's *Imitation of Christ*, John Foxe's *Book of Martyrs*, John Bunyan's *Pilgrim's Progress*, and John Milton's *Paradise Lost*. To these, we should add volumes of sermons – those of Jonathan Edwards, for example, John Wesley, and George Whitefield, among many others. Then there were commentaries on the Bible. Perhaps the best known of these were those of Thomas Scott (1747–1821), an English Calvinist whose Commentary on the Bible appeared in a weekly series from 1788 to 1792. There were also a great number of religious pamphlets and tracts, poured out by Evangelical printing presses on both sides of the Atlantic. There were religious magazines and newspapers. And there were collections of hymns. Evangelicalism was a remarkably literate religious culture, which fed a great hunger for spiritual reading.

John Bunyan and Pilgrim's Progress

Evangelicalism certainly confirmed as well as challenged aspects of contemporary society. Its attitude toward women is salient here. Generally speaking, until the rise of modern feminism, Evangelicalism did not seriously question the prevailing attitudes toward the respective roles of men and women. In most of the denominations, men were the leaders. Some denominations did nevertheless expand the range of possibilities for women. In Primitive Methodism in Britain and America, for example, women could become lay preachers and class leaders for a time, though the onset of Victorian respectability tended to restrict this development. Significantly, it was from the Primitive Methodists, however, that the Salvation Army was to emerge, and its founder, William Booth's, wife Catherine (1829–90), was no passive, domestic Victorian woman. Catherine was a forceful and effective evangelist in her own right, and the Army was a pioneer of women's ministry, even though it also subscribed to the general view of male leadership. Another innovator was Ellen Ranyard (1809–79), creator of the "Bible Women" in London in the 1860s, an organization of Evangelical women who ministered to the poor, and particularly to women. Ranyard's example was followed in other cities in Britain and America, and encouraged the formation of new Evangelical organizations catering specifically for women. Despite variations between denominations, overall there was much consistency in the Evangelical approach to the role of women. Freedom from church tradition gave scope for women to acquire new roles and responsibilities formerly denied to them, but attention to the apparent sense of Scripture mostly kept women out of leadership roles.

There was also a common Evangelical language, which stretched across the various doctrinal divisions between the churches. Giving "testimony" of their conversion, all Evangelicals would describe their former lives in such a way as to emphasize their sinful living, their living in darkness, and their "lost" condition. Sometimes the sins they had actually committed might seem minor, but they were magnified by contrast with their realization of God's saving grace. The process of conversion itself was frequently described in sudden and dramatic terms, with all the emphasis on God's initiative. Usually this came at a meeting, when the unwilling sinner had been cajoled along by someone else, or had been accustomed to go but had had a "hard heart." But God's agency was not seen as something abstract. It was intensely personal. And it was above all to be described through the personalism of real encounter with Jesus Christ. Evangelicals were comfortable with a familiarity about Jesus that other Christians found disturbing. "What a friend we have in Jesus, all our sins and griefs to bear" ran the popular mid-nineteenth century hymn written in 1855 by the Irish-born, Canadian resident Joseph Medlicott Scriven (1819–86). Scriven's sentiments were nothing new. They had been shared by Evangelicals for over a hundred years. After conversion followed a transformed life, marked above all by joy, suffused with the sense of assurance of God's salvation of

Charles Haddon Spurgeon

the sinner through Jesus Christ. In Methodism, this assurance led, as we have seen, into the doctrine of perfection. In other forms of Evangelicalism, including Evangelical Calvinism, it might lead to a constant watch on one's motives and actions, with a disciplined attention to the Bible.

Many of these elements are present in countless conversion stories, recounted in magazines and autobiographies throughout the late eighteenth and nineteenth centuries. One example will perhaps suffice here. It is the conversion of one of the most famous English Baptist ministers of the nineteenth century, Charles Haddon Spurgeon (1834–92). Taken from Spurgeon's biography, it captures powerfully the depth of despair of a sinner, and the extraordinary sense of release the realization of God's grace could bring:

> I was miserable, I could do scarcely anything. My heart was broken to pieces. Six months did I pray, prayed agonizingly with all my heart, and never had an answer. I resolved that in the town where I lived I would visit every place of worship, in order to find the way of salvation. I felt I was willing to do anything if God would only forgive me . . . At last, one snowy day, I found rather an obscure street and turned down a court, and there was a little chapel. I wanted to go somewhere, but I did not know this street. It was the Primitive Methodists' chapel. I had heard of this people from many, and how they sang so loudly that they made people's heads ache; but that did not matter. I wanted to know how I might be saved, and if they made my head ache ever so much, I did not care. So sitting down, the service went on, but no minister came. At last a very thin-looking man came into the pulpit. He opened the Bible and read these words: "Look unto me and be ye saved, all ye ends of the earth." Just setting his eyes upon me, as if he knew me all by heart, he said: "Young man, you are in trouble!" Well,

> I was, sure enough. Says he: "You will never get out of it unless you look to Christ." Then, lifting his eyes, he cried, as only a Primitive Methodist could do, "Look, look, look!" I saw at once the way of salvation. O, how I did leap for joy at that moment! I know not what else he said, I was so possessed with that one thought . . . I looked until I could almost have looked my eyes away, and in heaven I will look on still, in my joy unspeakable.[1]

Yet how was it that this intense experience of Christ, with its characteristic contrast of despair and joy, had come to typify Protestantism?

Revivalism in the New World

We shall look first of all at North America, where the emotional energy of revivalism was most unfettered. Ironically, the very success of Evangelicalism here replaced the half-hearted colonial establishments with a more pervasive, if unofficial, form of Protestant Christianity. The fathers of the American Revolution were, admittedly, mostly Deist, or at least professors of an unsectarian, liberal Christianity. On the grounds of religious liberty, and influenced by hostility to the Anglican or Episcopal Church's loyalty to Britain, they were determined that there would be no "state church" in the new United States. Yet the freedom this constitutional position afforded to all Christian denominations paradoxically increased religious competition and strengthened the overall hold of the churches on the population. By the early nineteenth century, many overseas visitors were noting that, in this land of religious freedom, a de facto Protestant establishment had come into being. A Philadelphia minister pointed out that this was evident in state laws requiring Sabbath observance, "proclamations calling the nation to prayer, court rulings in church cases, oathswearing on the Bible and the maintenance of chaplains in legislative halls and the armed services."[2]

The growth of revivalist Protestantism in America was due first and foremost to the Methodists. Whereas George Whitefield's preaching tours had stirred up congregations from earlier in the century, it was not until the 1770s that the Wesleys had organized preachers from England for the colonies. Francis Asbury (1745–1816) was the most indefatigable of these. Arriving in America in 1771, Asbury began a remarkable itinerant ministry, covering almost 300,000 miles on horseback before his death, westwards from the coast across the Appalachian Mountains, and northwards into Canada. Although Methodist growth was temporarily held up by the Wesleys' loyalty to the British Crown during the American Revolution, in 1784 the American Methodists were formally reorganized and provided with their own ministers. From then on, growth continued apace. Methodist theology, and Methodist emotionalism, open-air preaching, and classes, proved immensely popular, and it was flexible, too, as new societies could be started quickly in the rapidly expanding frontier towns. Methodist organization proved adaptable. By the middle of the nineteenth century, despite some internal divisions, the Methodist churches in America had come to be by far the most numerous single branch of Protestantism. In 1850, some 2.6 million Americans were Methodist church members, a figure representing over 34% of total church membership in America – a dramatic increase from the 2.5% estimated in 1776.[3]

Francis Asbury

Other denominations were close

behind the Methodists, however. In the West in the 1790s revivals began again, partly under the influence of the Presbyterian preacher James McGready (c.1758–1817). McGready took up the charge of three small churches in Logan County, Kentucky, in 1796. From there his work spread. In 1800, he assembled huge crowds at open-air meetings near the Gasper River, meetings that went on for several days at a time and were eventually to be called "camp meetings" – a term that crossed the ocean to Britain and was taken up by Methodist groups there. The "Second Awakening," as this period of revival was called, lasted until the 1830s. It was marked by the resurgence of emotional excess, with shouting, wailing, and sometimes even shaking during services, that many ministers in the eastern colonies had earlier condemned. But, as one historian has written, "[i]t was natural that frontier dwellers would demand this; that they would cry aloud in wrestling with their guilt, and that they would laugh and jump and shout with joy when they had purged their souls."[4] During this period, the Baptists began to emerge as the second most popular Protestant denomination after Methodism. Again, this was so particularly in the southern and western states. There were almost 200,000 Baptists in the United States in 1812; by 1850, this number had risen to over 1.6 million.[5]

Composite of famous preachers and evangelists including, top left, Charles Grandison Finney

Yet by far the most significant American revivalist of the first half of the nineteenth century was neither a Methodist nor a Baptist. Charles Grandison

Finney (1792–1875) came from a Presbyterian background in New England. Having undergone a powerful and dramatic conversion experience in 1821, while he was a legal apprentice, Finney rapidly became a compelling, immensely popular preacher. By 1831 he was a national figure, having conducted revivals in Rochester, Philadelphia, Boston, and New York. Eventually he broke from Presbyterianism, accusing it of neglecting too much the human capacity to seek redemption. Finney's was an essentially optimistic, buoyant message of hope for the sinner. Yet his major contribution to the development of revivalism in America was through his so-called "new measures." These were in fact not new at all, but a systematic exploitation of practices other revivalists had already begun to use. One was the "anxious bench," a row of seats specially reserved (usually at the front of the chapel or meeting hall, or just below the preacher's podium) on which were sat those who were to be admonished for their sins. Another was the "protracted meeting," a succession of nightly meetings, which had as their aim the precipitating of the anxious sinner into conversion. Finney's trademark became the deliberate manipulation of emotions, and encouragement of conversion, to the point at which those in fear of their spiritual state would be drawn to make a dramatic statement of their discovery of faith. It is from Finney in particular that the modern practice of calling out those who want to be saved from the body of the meeting is derived. Finney, then, marked a new development in popular revivalism – the intensification of organized measures to the point where revivalism, rather than being a somewhat chaotic and spontaneous result of revivalist preaching, could be regularized and practiced almost as a mechanical discipline.

For all his popularity, his mesmerizing pulpit oratory, and his development of revivalist techniques, Finney was also symptomatic of a gathering crisis in American Protestantism. For Finney was, like so many Protestant preachers from the north, an unapologetic opponent of slavery. And the slave issue increasingly divided Protestants in the first half of the nineteenth century. The division did not always run on geographical lines. Yet the most serious splits did roughly correspond – not surprisingly, given the massive influence Protestantism had achieved over American culture and public life – to that between the Union and the Confederacy in the Civil War. Perhaps most seriously affected were the Baptists and the Methodists. Baptist missionary agencies, particularly sponsored and supported from the north, increasingly objected to recognizing members who owned slaves. This prompted the withdrawal of support by many of the southern Baptist churches, and in the end, in 1845, the formation of the Southern Baptist Convention. Southern Baptists were not, it should be emphasized, automatic defenders of the institution of slavery, but they were at this time defenders of the freedom of church members to own slaves if they wished. Even so, on other theological grounds many Baptists refused to join the Southern Convention, and formed their own, smaller networks of Baptist churches. Similar divisions opened up in the Methodist churches, and then in the Presbyterian, Lutheran, and Episcopalian churches.

A group of 'modern' preachers and writers including (bearded in the oval frame, top centre) Dwight L Moody

Moreover, the number of black church members had been rising from the end of the eighteenth century. Divisions within the churches over slavery often encouraged the formation of separate, black-led churches. The African Methodist Episcopal Church, founded by the former slave Richard Allen (1760–1831) was one of the first of these. Allen was ordained as a Methodist deacon in 1799 after years of conflict with white church trustees, having established Bethel Church as a black church in 1793. Further struggles over the control of church property ensued, and eventually Allen felt obliged to draw other black Methodist churches into the creation of their own denomination in 1814. Other black denominations followed suit. Black Baptist churches were formed across the United States, though particularly in the North. In 1845, their permanent existence was symbolized by the formation of the African Baptist Missionary Society. In the South, though repression and of course the widespread existence of slavery inhibited the emergence of black churches at first, still some did come into being, such as the First African Baptist Church of Savannah, Georgia, at the end of the eighteenth century. Perhaps the most fitting comment on the position of black Christianity in America is that of a recent historian:

> No group stood as far outside America's dominant pattern of religion between the Revolution and the Civil War as the slaves. It is a testimony to their resilience as well as to the transforming power of Christianity that a religion used so often to support the slave system could become a means of counteracting its inhuman influence.[6]

By the middle of the nineteenth century, Evangelical Protestantism dominated the religious scene in America. Its characteristic expression, however, was not Charles Finney, for all his fame, but a pair of revivalists who, operating often as a team, carried the message of American revivalism across the ocean to Britain. Dwight Lyman Moody (1837–99) was a New England businessman who, after his conversion, used his formidable powers of organization and salesmanship to promote religious revival. Like all salesmen, Moody had a simple message, which he presented as the "3 R's": "Ruin" by sin, "Redemption" by Jesus Christ, and "Regeneration"

Thomas Chalmers

through the work of the Holy Spirit. His motivation was equally simple. As he famously said, "I look upon this world as a wrecked vessel. God has given me a lifeboat and said to me, 'Moody, save all you can'."[7] It was the songs of Ira Sankey (1840–1908) that made the duo particularly famous, for if Moody's preaching was inimitable, Sankey's songs could be circulated and used again and again. Sankey himself led the singing that invariably began one of Moody's evangelistic meetings: "[t]he informality and good spirits generated by audience participation helped to unify the crowd and to focus the attention of all the participants on the service that followed."[8] Moody and Sankey toured Britain from 1873 to 1875, and raised huge crowds and excitement. Returning to America, they became the focus of a new wave of urban revivals. Yet Moody's influence also encompassed permanent institutions. He founded what became the Moody Bible Institute in Chicago, and, in 1876, the Student Volunteer Movement, later to become a worldwide network of societies aimed at galvanizing young people's commitment to Christian mission.

Over the border in Canada, religious life was also touched by the rise of Evangelical Protestantism. In the province of Quebec at this period, Roman Catholicism was dominant. Elsewhere, the established Anglican Church remained proportionately more popular and influential than was its Episcopal equivalent in the United States. Yet there was a diversity of free churches that echoed the growing religious pluralism of Britain as well as the United States. Scottish Presbyterians settled in large numbers in the eastern provinces. One of them, Thomas McCulloch (1776–1843) founded Pictou Academy in 1816, and became a leading light in Canadian Evangelical Protestantism. Methodism grew apace in the eastern provinces, too. Further west, Ontario became, by the mid-nineteenth century,

William Wilberforce

Canada's largest province in terms of population. Methodists and Presbyterians came to outnumber the Anglicans, and Baptists were the largest of a number of minority traditions. There was much contact between the Canadian churches and churches in the United States, until the War of 1812 engineered a decisive shift in Canadian national identity away from its more powerful southern neighbor. As a result, Canadian church life began to evolve its own distinctive ethos, more "disciplined" or restrained than the life of many American churches, with the Evangelical theology characteristic of most Protestantism of this period nevertheless rarely expressed with the emotional exuberance of the myriad revivalists further south. Gradually, the influence of Anglicanism faded. But co-operation between Protestant churches, rather than vigorous competition, became much more characteristic of Canadian church life.

Evangelicalism in the Old World

In Britain, the fact that there were established churches in Scotland, and in England, Wales, and Ireland was bound to affect the way Evangelical Protestantism developed. In Scotland, the Presbyterian establishment of the Church of Scotland was more dominant, proportionately, than was its Anglican sister across the border in England. There were free churches, but they were mostly small. Evangelicalism developed within the Scottish establishment as a more energetic and radical force than the rather dry, Calvinist "orthodoxy" characteristic of Scottish religion in the late eighteenth and early nineteenth centuries. Its most famous representative was Thomas Chalmers (1780–1847). A mathematician by background, Chalmers was an enormously impressive, energetic man, who pioneered a systematic approach to urban mission in his years as minister of parishes in Glasgow from 1815 to 1823. He revived parish schools, began regular visiting, built new churches, and organized a system of elders and deacons to undertake parish work. His aim was to regenerate urban life through the conversion and transformation of the lives of the poor. His was an established church strategy: through a "proper parochial system," he argued, "legal poor relief could be eliminated and social harmony restored."[9] But Chalmers' vision ran into difficulties when it implied that the believing community of a local church should have priority in its choice of minister over the rights of legal "patrons" (those who owned the right of appointment as a matter of property). The resulting conflict between "Evangelicals" and "orthodox" parties led to the division of the Scottish church in 1843, when Chalmers and his Evangelical supporters left the establishment to create the Free Church of Scotland.

In England, Wales, and Ireland, after the loss of the Methodists, no later division in the Anglican establishment took place over the rise of Evangelicalism. Instead, from the last quarter of the century, a gradual development took place of Evangelical principles within the established Church. This was quite different in ethos from Methodism, however. Many of its supporters, for one thing, were moderate Calvinists. They did not share the Wesleys' conviction that salvation was offered to all, and were suspicious of the Methodist emphasis on an attainable Christian perfection. But they recognized, with the Wesleys, a need to revitalize the faith of Anglicans. One of their leaders was a layman, William Wilberforce (1759–1833), who in 1797 published *A Practical View of the Prevailing Religious System of Professed Christians*, a book that for all the clumsiness of its title represented an excoriating attack on the emptiness and formalism of much contemporary Anglican church life. Wilberforce in a way was typical of the new Anglican Evangelical leadership. Socially and politically conservative, he relied on a principle of leadership that largely assumed the continuation of social deference in a highly status-conscious society. He was a member of Parliament, and mixed mostly with the educated elite. He and his like were transforming Anglicanism "from above." They were not, mostly, interested in popular revivalism, being suspicious of emotional excess and its chaotic effects. His clerical counterpart and exact contemporary was Charles Simeon (1759–1836), for over 50 years vicar of Holy Trinity church in Cambridge. Simeon saw his task as the training-up of a new generation of Evangelical undergraduates, many of whom became clergymen. In this gradual transformation of Anglicanism, the very structure of the established church aided Evangelicals. Through the system of private patronage, they could buy up (or create, for new churches) the power to appoint Evangelical clergy to parish churches. Their influence then began to extend throughout the country, as the numbers of Evangelical clergymen grew.

Yet Evangelicalism was not without its challenging aspects for contemporary society. The most obvious of these was its campaign against slavery. Wilberforce was instrumental in this. With a group of like-minded Evangelical clergy and laity, many of whom lived in and around his home village of Clapham in south London, and so attracted the nickname "the Clapham Sect," Wilberforce orchestrated a campaign of sustained parliamentary criticism of slavery in the British colonies, and of the slave trade. Anglican Evangelicals were well supported in this by Evangelical Dissenters – those Methodists, Baptists, Independents or Congregationalists, Quakers, and Presbyterians, many of whom were descendents of those who had been forced out of the national church during the seventeenth-century crisis. The formation of local abolitionist societies, mostly dominated by Evangelical Anglicans and Dissenters, was accompanied by the presentation of petitions to Parliament. After years of obstruction from vested interests, Wilberforce achieved the abolition of the slave trade in 1807. But complete abolition of slavery in the British colonies had to wait until right at the end of his life, with the passage of the Emancipation Act in 1833.

The campaign against the slave trade was the most startling and symbolic Evangelical social crusade in Britain. But it was expressed by a wider determination to transform British society from within. Resisting the political radicalism that had been stirred up in Britain by sympathizers with the French Revolution of 1789, Evangelicals both emphasized the divinely ordained nature of social hierarchy, and urged on the rich and influential their responsibility to assist the poor. In this highly conservative sense, Evangelicalism sought to reform society. Wilberforce had founded, in 1787, a Society for the Reformation of Manners. Just as in America, Evangelicals in Britain supported the restriction of gaming, and work, on Sundays. They promoted the building of new churches, and schools. The Sunday School movement in particular was sponsored by Evangelical Anglicans and Dissenters alike. The distribution of Bibles and of improving literature was encouraged through the formation of the Religious Tract Society in 1799 and the Bible Society in 1803. Later still, Evangelicals came to the fore as critics of cruelty to animals, and as advocates of temperance. Under the forceful Evangelical aristocrat, Anthony Ashley Cooper (1801–85), the 7th Earl of Shaftesbury, Evangelicals became prominent in campaigns to improve working conditions in the new industrial towns and cities, imposing maximum working hours, restricting the employment of women and children, and promoting the building of improved housing for the laboring poor.

By the middle of the nineteenth century, British Evangelicalism, in its Anglican, Scottish Presbyterian, and Dissenting forms, had achieved a remarkable change in the ethos of Victorian culture. Its commitment to social amelioration had borne fruit in a rising number of legislative initiatives, and in the creation of an extensive network of social institutions, including churches, schools, and charities. It had transformed the values of all classes of society. Gone, mostly, was the conspicuous and reckless spending and easy morality of the years of the Regency. Churchgoing

Anthony Ashley Cooper, 7th Earl of Shaftesbury

was fashionable. Victorian family life was restrained, "respectable," and self-consciously moral. Regular family prayers and Bible-reading were common. If the poor did not often go to church regularly – particularly in the cities – nevertheless many of them did at some time in their lives, and they shared in the widespread, common Evangelical culture of the period, with its strong concept of duty, and its somewhat sentimentalized picture of Jesus. The Bible remained the most popular book in the Victorian home.

1 Taken from H. L. Wayland, *Charles H Spurgeon, His Faith and Works*, on http://ourworld.compuserve.com/homepages/Brad_Haugaard/spconver.htm

2 T. L. Smith, *Revivalism and Social Reform in Mid-Nineteenth Century America* (Abingdon Press, New York, 1957), p. 34.

3 R. Finke & R. Stark, 'How the Upstart Sects Won America: 1776–1850', Journal for the Scientific Study of Religion, 28 (1989), p. 31.

4 K. J. Hardman, *Charles Grandison Finney 1792–1875*. Revivalist and Reformer (Syracuse University Press, New York, 1987), p. 9.

5 Finke & Stark, op. cit.

6 Noll, op. cit., p. 205.

7 Cited in ibid., p. 289.

8 J. F. Findlay, *Dwight L. Moody. American Evangelist 1837–1899* (University of Chicago Press, Chicago, 1969), p. 209.

9 S. J. Brown, *The National Churches of England, Ireland and Scotland 1801–1846* (Oxford University Press, Oxford, 2001), p. 82.

Chapter 5
CATHOLICS AND HERETICS

FOR CENTURIES AFTER the Reformation, in western Europe and North America there were only two kinds of people – Catholics and Protestants. Catholics lived under the direction of a worldwide church, centered on Rome. Though this church contained many different countries and peoples within it, it had a common language for services – Latin – and a common law, or "canon law." It was a uniform organization, with the same basic structure of ministry and the same basic discipline in every country. On the other hand, there were as many varieties of Protestantism as there were countries. Nothing really held different Protestant countries together apart from their suspicion of Catholicism. All that the word "Protestant" meant, in fact, was one who protests against the Pope's authority. It did not signify any great bond of unity between churches. Protestants disagreed bitterly with each other on many things, including church teaching and organization.

These two great communities of faith looked at each other with deep suspicion. To Protestants, Catholicism looked like a hostile, secret power reaching through world, with the Pope as the sinister figure at the center of the spider's web. Catholics could not be trusted to give their first loyalty to the State, since they owed it to the Pope. Worse, they had departed from pure Christian teaching. They had elevated Jesus' mother Mary into an object of devotion in her own right. This was surely idolatry? They had compromised the power of faith, by teaching the doctrine of merit – believers could perform "good works" and so procure salvation for themselves. They had abandoned the authority of the Bible, and placed their trust in the all-too-human authority of the Pope and the cardinals.

This Protestant criticism of Catholicism ran very deep indeed in North America and in northern Europe. The expansiveness of America to some extent promoted grudging harmony and tolerance, since it was always possible to move further out to start a new church or congregation. Here, then, anti-Catholicism proved to be much less dangerous to social stability than it was in Britain. In Canada, as early as 1774 – long before this was possible in Britain – the British Government

The Gordon Riots in 1780 led to the destruction of several Roman Catholic chapels and private houses.

had adopted a policy of guaranteeing freedom of worship and protection to Catholics in French-speaking areas, after British success in the Seven Years' War had led to the complete conquest of formerly French colonies there. Despite opposition from the American colonies further south, the policy proved successful. In the American War of Independence, Canadian Catholics supported the King. But in Britain, Catholicism remained the object of deep suspicion. In 1780, attempts by the British government to reduce anti-Catholic legislation prompted opposition from the Protestant Association of Lord George Gordon. In the "Gordon riots" that ensued, Catholic chapels were destroyed in London, priests and other "papists" were attacked, hundreds of properties were damaged, and the disorder ended only by the intervention of the army.

To Catholics, Protestants were dangerous heretics and "schismatics," or breakers away from the true Church. They were untrustworthy, since they did not recognize proper obedience to the authority of the Church. They valued their own opinion – or "private judgment" – above the traditions of the Church. They claimed to value the Bible, but they all disagreed with each other about how it was to be interpreted. Their freedom would lead – Catholics contended – to social disorder. Protestants, in abandoning the Church, had ceased to be true Christians. To the Catholic mind, Protestants were heretics, worse even than infidels. Protestantism was but a short step to atheism and moral degeneracy. In Catholic countries, rulers had gradually adopted "Enlightened" values, and persecution had given way mostly to limited toleration. But this was not a particularly difficult policy. Protestantism had all but disappeared from the Catholic countries of southern Europe, driven out by persecution in an earlier age. The exceptions were the German states, where a permanent division between Catholic and Protestant communities had come into being since the Peace of Westphalia in 1648.

Yet, even though full of suspicion about each other, Protestants and Catholics did share a great deal in common. Both communities saw their own form of religion as a necessary support for government and social order. Christianity promoted human well-being. True Christians made good citizens. Without religion, society would fall apart. Christianity defended the traditional hierarchies of Europe, and the colonial governments that had come into being in America. Everywhere in Europe it was universally assumed that governments would protect and privilege particular churches, because the interests of Church and State were bound up together.

All of that was to change dramatically at the end of the eighteenth century and the beginning of the nineteenth century. A series of social and political crises in America and Europe was to bring much of the older way of seeing the Church's role crashing down. To the long-established division of western society into Catholic and Protestant communities, a completely new principle of division was to be added, and that was a political one. This was no less than a revolution in Christianity and its place in society, and it prompted a new wave of revival – this time, a Catholic one.

Revolution in the new and old worlds

When the Thirteen Colonies declared themselves independent from Britain in 1776, no one – least of all the colonists themselves – thought that they were about to launch a social revolution. They were not seeking to turn the world upside down, but to secure their livelihoods, their families' security and prosperity, against the taxation and legal power of the Crown. But ending the link between the colonies and the monarch did at once raise the question of religion, because the privileged status of the Church of England had been carried into the colonies by the British. At first, the rebels, or "patriots" as they came to be called, avoided damaging statements about any future religious policy. Many Catholics and Episcopalians supported the patriotic cause.

But the creation of the new American constitution was another matter. Its making brought to the fore Thomas Jefferson (1743–1826) and James Madison (1751–1836), authors of the constitution, who both shared in the now fashionable

Thomas Jefferson

James Madison

"Enlightenment" suspicion of traditional Christianity, though they both also claimed to be followers of the true spirit of Christianity. Jefferson, Anglican by upbringing, went so far as to call the Bible a "ground work of vulgar ignorance, of things impossible, of superstitions, fanaticisms, and fabrications," but claimed also that "I am a real Christian." Madison was more respectful of the traditional churches than Jefferson, but still an "ardent champion" of religious liberty and of the separation of Church and State. Under their influence, supported by others, the First Amendment, effected in 1791, disallowed government support of a particular church, and enshrined full religious liberty in the new constitution. In the long run, this was to set the scene for the massive expansion and diversification of Christianity in America. Removed from political controversy, both Catholic and Protestant churches were unfettered. Relying solely on their own supporters' income, the churches moved into a position of open competition with each other. With a rapidly growing population, and an expanding hinterland, America in the nineteenth and early twentieth centuries came to be a land of opportunity for the churches.

Things did not work out the same way in Europe. Here, by far the most dramatic event of the period was the French Revolution, which had altogether more sinister implications for Christianity. The Revolution that broke out in 1789 rapidly moved in an increasingly radical direction. The Catholic Church in France was reformed by the new government, but many of the clergy refused to accept the oath to the new constitution, and so the Church was split. Persecution of the "non-juring" clergy followed. Then, in the years of "terror," when the king and many other opponents of the Revolution were executed, Christianity itself came under attack. The government tried to suppress it, and rival "cults" such as that of the "Supreme Being," and even that of "Reason," were begun, though they never really took off. The message to the rest of Europe seemed clear enough. Revolution was anti-Christian. Destroy the Church, and you would destroy the very fabric of traditional society. The mob would rule. All across Europe, not only monarchs, but all those who had much to lose from social revolution were afraid. Yet the principles of Revolution, expressed in the Revolutionary "trinity" of liberty, fraternity, and equality, were carried throughout Europe by radical sympathizers, and above all by war. The Revolutionary Wars that engulfed Europe from 1792 were swiftly followed by the wars of Napoleon. Napoleon cast himself as a child of the Revolution. He was not anti-religious, but he was a religious skeptic, and valued Christianity only so far as he could use it to strengthen his rule.

The effect of the French Revolution on Europe was incalculable. It represented by far the greatest crisis in Christianity in Europe since the Reformation. And it particularly affected Catholic countries – France, Spain, Italy, and parts of the Austrian Empire. The Revolution could not be cast as a Protestant development. It was the offspring of a Catholic culture. If European Catholicism had gone a little stale in the eighteenth century, as many of its leading clergy succumbed to the moderate, easy-going "Enlightened" Christianity of their age, the Revolution came as an enormous shock. It suggested that there was no accommodation to be sought with progressive values. Instead, Catholicism had to rediscover itself, to be confident about itself, and determined to recover its hold on the people of Europe. It had to find a way of acting once more as the social cement that held the whole edifice of society together. This was the ambition of a generation of Catholic writers – especially French – who included Louis De Bonald (1754–1840), Joseph de Maistre (1754–1821) and Felicité Robert de Lamennais (1782–1854). But it was an ambition not for writers alone, but for all Catholics. Behind all of the Catholic activism of the nineteenth century lay the ghost of Revolution.

Catholic revivalism

The chance came with the end of the Napoleonic era after the battle of Waterloo in 1815. Political stability was short-lived, as nineteenth-century Europe was riven by the continued threat of revolution, by civil wars, and by the rise of nationalism. Moreover the papacy was on the defensive, weakened by successive occupations of Italy. The papacy was financially dependent on the Papal States, the territories governed (and taxed) directly by the Pope. The movement for Italian unification was to have dire implications for it, because it sought to strip the papacy of these territories. The scope for concerted papal action was limited, and the revitalization of European Catholicism came about largely through local initiatives, albeit with support from the papacy.

In France, for example, with the restoration of the monarchy in 1815 came the chance for the Catholic Church to begin to reassert its position in the countryside. It did not have the extensive lands it had owned before the Revolution, but it continued to have its clergy paid by the State, as had been settled by the Concordat Napoleon had concluded with the papacy in 1801. The monastic orders had been proscribed during the Revolution, their monasteries destroyed or turned over for State use as prisons, workhouses, and such like. Now, they began to return and found new communities. The missionary orders played a key part in the re-evangelization of French society. The Redemptorists, for example, originally founded in 1732 by Alphonsus Maria Liguori (1696–1787), were particularly active in France. The Jesuits, re-founded in 1814 by Pope Pius VII, were instrumental in establishing schools, and in pastoral visitation. New Catholic parishes were founded, or old parishes were revitalized. In the towns, too, the vigor of Catholic religion was everywhere in evidence. Epidemics in particular provided a vital opportunity both for pastoral visitation, and for intercessory prayer. In Marseille, during the cholera epidemic of 1834–5, for example, the populace demanded the return of Catholic processions, banned by the city council years earlier. A huge open-air Mass was held in the city center, and one estimate was that some 30,000 people were "prostrated before the holy mysteries and even the windows of all the adjoining houses [were] filled with spectators on their knees."[1]

In America, too, it was the religious orders that were the main source of Catholic revival. The Redemptorists arrived in America in 1832. A handful of Jesuit priests already in America were supplemented by the arrival of numbers expelled from France after the 1830 Revolution. Another order of preachers, the Vincentians, originally founded in France by Vincent de Paul (1580–1660), was also active in America. The main means by which Catholic revival was propagated, both in American and Europe, was the parish mission. This was a short, intensive period of preaching, teaching, and visiting, sometimes no more than a week at a time, in which several itinerant priests would usually combine to lift the spiritual life of a parish or area. Like Protestant revivalism, it was a technique that lent itself to the dispersed nature of American settlers' lives, though it could also be used in the concentrated conditions of the city. Unlike Protestant revivalism, however, its focus was particularly on the sacramental means of grace – on baptizing families, on hearing confession and giving absolution, and above all on the Mass. Parish missions were first held in America before the end of the eighteenth century, but they did not become common until the 1840s, when the numbers of mission priests seriously increased. In the 1850s, according to one modern historian, "the mission phenomenon spread like wild fire."[2]

Yet Catholic revival happened not only because of the remarkable efforts of the religious orders. It was also the product of patterns of population growth and immigration, and here there is a similar story to be told about Britain and America. In America, at the beginning of the nineteenth century, the Catholic population was

Basilica of the Assumption, Baltimore

small and scattered. In 1815, there were only around 150,000 Catholics, spread across the states. There were a few areas of concentration, such as Baltimore, where the first Catholic cathedral in America, the Basilica of the Assumption, was built between 1804 and 1818. But mostly parishes were poor, priests were few, and there was a great deal of "leakage," the loss of Catholics to Protestant churches or to religious indifference because of the lack of proper church provision. The Catholic presence was particularly weak in the deep South. In Alabama and Florida, for example, out of some 344,000 people in 1830, only 8,000 were Catholics. Yet from the 1830s onwards, the growth of the Catholic population of America was phenomenal. Fed above all by migration from Europe, it had grown to over 1.6 million by 1850, and almost doubled again in ten years alone. At first, migration was from Ireland (especially after the potato famine of 1846) and from Germany, but later in the nineteenth century settlers from southern and eastern Europe, including Italy and Poland, also arrived in great numbers. Some 700,000 Italians emigrated to America in the 1890s, and over 2 million in the 1900s. Soon, the Catholic population of America constituted the single largest Christian denomination, outstripping even the Methodists. It grew everywhere, but especially in the northeast and the mid-west. By 1910, there were over 15 million Catholics in the United States.

In Britain, the growth of the Catholic community in the nineteenth century was also considerable. At the beginning of the century, there was a small, native Catholic population in England and Wales, a residue largely of the "recusant" families of the sixteenth and seventeenth centuries – those families which had conscientiously refused to embrace the Anglican religious settlement and had remained faithful to the "old religion." One historian has estimated the size of this population as around 80,000, out of around 9 million people.[3] By 1851, when the one and only national religious census of church attendance was undertaken, this number had swelled to perhaps around 380,000. It was to climb further still, as the century wore on. And the source of this growth once again was immigration, mostly just from Ireland. By 1851, over half a million residents of England and Wales had been born in Ireland. Since Ireland was a country of great Catholic strength, it is not surprising that the English Catholic church came, in the course of the nineteenth century, to feel so much an outpost of the Irish church. Moreover, unlike America, where Catholic migrants were as likely to settle in the frontier as in the cities, in Britain Irish Catholicism was almost exclusively urban. Cities such as Liverpool, Manchester, Glasgow, and, of course, London, had large and often densely concentrated Irish communities.

The challenges were similar on both sides of the Atlantic. Rapidly growing Catholic populations demanded an equally rapid response from the Church, if the faithful were not to fall prey to "leakage." Churches had to be built quickly. Clergy had to be recruited in ever-increasing numbers. The faithful had to be bound into the Church by administration of the sacraments, and by Catholic teaching in schools, Sunday schools, and churches. The religious orders were particularly adept at mission and educational work. Priestly celibacy, so often claimed today to be a significant discouragement to the recruitment of clergy, was an advantage in the mission conditions of the nineteenth century. Celibate clergy were cheap, bringing no family to support with them. They were also bound by close bonds of obedience to their superiors in the hierarchy. Their ethos was one of self-sacrificial service of their communities. Moreover, they were also relatively unencumbered at first by ties to the established political and social elites. They were not embarrassed by the use of techniques that some of their Protestant rivals might regard as "vulgar" – by processions, by vivid and dramatic mission meetings, by the use of stirring music. The theology of Catholicism was naturally very different from that of Protestant Evangelicalism. It emphasized the role of the Church in mediating salvation to the believer in a way that was foreign to many Protestants. Yet it too could speak of the abject condition of the sinner, of imminent judgment, and of the need for repentance and conversion. It too could urge on repentant sinners the abandonment of a life of drink, gambling, and violence. Catholic clergy, like their Protestant counterparts, projected Christianity as the ultimate protector of the family and the home. They supported the temperance movement, forming their own temperance organizations. And they also supported, like Protestants, a great penumbra of charities. Just as intensely as Protestants, Catholics envisaged their religion as the means to a revitalization of society as a whole.

A culture of devotion

Yet what is striking about this emergent Catholic culture in Britain and America is its uniformity. Despite the very great social and geographical differences between communities within the United States and Britain, and despite the variety of national backgrounds to be encountered in American Catholicism in particular, Roman Catholicism in this period demonstrated a remarkable identity of ethos. Threatened by what they perceived as the destructive character of political radicalism, nationalism, and liberalism, Catholics emphasized the central hierarchy and authority of the Catholic Church. "Ultramontanism" ("beyond the mountains") was the name given to the policy of extending the authority of the papacy throughout the Catholic world. The more nationalist instincts of some parts of the Church – such as the French church – were to be suppressed, in the interests of affirming the essential unity and identity of Catholic worship and teaching. It is easy to cast this as the menacing advance of a centralizing machine. But that would be a mistake. The papacy was exceptionally weak in this period. The diminution of the Papal States in the 1860s, culminating in their final loss in 1870 when French troops withdrew from Rome, left the papacy exposed financially and vulnerable politically. Under Pius IX, Pope from 1846 to 1878, this declining political force was compensated by the determination to preserve the integrity of the Church's teaching and life against the prevailing secular culture. The pinnacle of this policy was the first Vatican Council of 1869 to 1870, which declared the doctrine of papal infallibility.

Pope Pius IX

There were devotional aspects of this policy, too. One was Pius IX's declaration of the dogma of the Immaculate Conception in 1854. This doctrine holds that the Blessed Virgin Mary, though conceived by a father and mother in the usual human way, was preserved by God from the stain of original sin, so that she could be the immaculate bearer of Jesus Christ. The dogma had been held by some within

Catholicism for many centuries, but also disputed by others. Pius's declaration was an assertion of a distinctive strain within Catholic piety. It marked a certain Catholic confidence and vigor. It also marked a renewed devotion centered on Mary herself.

No better example of this new "ultramontane" piety can perhaps be given than the cult of Lourdes. On 11 February 1858, a poor fourteen-year-old girl, Bernadette Soubirous, went with two friends to look for wood, on the outskirts of the Pyrennean town of Lourdes. She sat down near a grotto, at the base of rocky outcrop, and took off her stockings. She heard the sound of a wind, and, looking up, saw a soft light in the grotto, and then a beautiful, smiling child in white. The child produced a rosary, and made the sign of the cross, and then disappeared. Bernadette had eighteen visions in all, watched by growing numbers of people. The thirteenth vision, on 2 March, brought a message from the child: "Go and tell the priests to come here on procession and to build a chapel."[4] But the local priest was skeptical, and said she should ask the child who she was. By now, the future "mission" of Lourdes was becoming clear through the visions: prayer, penitence, bathing and drinking in a fountain, processions, and a chapel. But the child did not respond to Bernadette's question until the feast of the Annunciation, 25 March, when, with crowds already forming, she eventually put her hands together, looked heavenwards and said "Que soy Immaculada Councepciou," "I am the Immaculate Conception." The visions ceased finally when the local authorities barred access to the site.

The Virgin Mary appears to Bernadette Soubirous

Whatever one thinks of this event, it was to become one of the most significant developments in popular Catholicism in the nineteenth century. Almost immediately after the visions had ceased, the happenings there became a battleground between the local Catholic hierarchy, inclined to skepticism about Bernadette's visions, and the Ultramontane press in France and the papacy itself. That it was a vision of the Immaculate Conception – Pius's declared dogma – naturally inclined the papacy toward support of the cult. The local clergy's suspicion, attacked by the press, became a pretext for the reform of French Catholicism. Pilgrimages on an increasingly national and then international scale were encouraged as the years went by. A highly ambitious church-building scheme was put in place in Lourdes, culminating in the construction of an enormous basilica in the 1870s and 1880s. Even that proved too small in the twentieth century, and was eventually supplemented in the 1950s by an underground, concrete church that can hold some 20,000 people. Bernadette herself died young, in a convent, and was eventually canonized in 1933. In the meantime, Lourdes had grown into perhaps the most famous center of pilgrimage in the modern world. Numbers visiting it swelled after miracle cures were reported there in the early 1870s. Today, Lourdes receives over six million pilgrims a year.

Lourdes was symptomatic of the adaptability of Catholicism. Despite its resistance to significant currents of modern thought, Roman Catholicism was adept at using characteristic features of its devotional culture to promote Catholicism in the modern world. If the religious orders were so often the instrument of Catholic revivalism, and the parish mission the means, the content included many distinctive or traditional aspects of Catholicism that were to prove remarkably attractive to modern society. Marian devotion was central to this. Promulgation of the doctrine of the Immaculate Conception was to be followed almost a century later by that of the Virgin's Assumption into heaven. Mary was a powerful symbol of the Catholic Church's appeal particularly to women, and to motherhood and the family. The cult of the saints was also enduring, and enabled the Catholic Church to highlight local or reasonably familiar figures who could be held up as an example to the faithful – Bernadette Soubirous herself, for example, or Jean-Baptiste-Marie Vianney (1786–1859), otherwise known as the "cure d'Ars," whose unstinting work as a parish priest and confessor later led to his canonization, or Therese of Lisieux (1873–97), the young Carmelite nun whose letters and autobiography gave a poignant insight into her faith and suffering. The cult of the Sacred Heart of Jesus proved to be another distinctive aspect of Catholic tradition that proved remarkably popular. And the Catholic Church was sustained by a network of national and international institutions every bit as powerful as those of Protestantism – newspapers, journals, schools, universities, lay societies ("sodalities," "confraternities"). The Catholic Church even developed in some countries rival associations to those of the secular trades unions. These were, unsurprisingly, strongest in predominantly Catholic countries, such as Spain and Italy, but they achieved some significant membership in America, too. More recently, in the twentieth century, the Catholic Church has absorbed elements of the charismatic revival.

In the contemporary world, nothing has come to symbolize the adaptability of Catholicism, however, as much as the Second Vatican Council. Summoned by Pope John XXIII in 1962, as it met over the next three years it developed into a re-commitment of the Catholic Church to its mission to proclaim and embody the gospel of Jesus Christ. Vatican II has been seen by many as an almost revolutionary departure from a static, formalistic Church practice. But that is an exaggeration. For one thing, as we have seen, the Catholic Church was far from dying. It was growing substantially throughout the twentieth century, especially in Africa and Asia. It was capable of developing new forms of popular piety. For another thing, there were signs of a new spirit of self-examination, and a new readiness to acknowledge organizational difficulties and weaknesses, in the years before the Council met. But above all, the Council was a moment of renewal. It did not simply reject out of hand all that the Church had been saying and doing. Indeed, it claimed to be rediscovering the true spirit of Catholicism, the spirit that had lain there all along but had sometimes been obscured by defensiveness and clericalism. This spirit was firmly rooted in the Bible. Vatican II was an attempt to reinvigorate the Catholic Church's understanding of the mission of Jesus Christ, and its own role in sustaining and prolonging that mission. It was a return to the theme of the servant Church, with less emphasis on the Church triumphant. With the servant Church came humility, and a new readiness to recognize the sincerity of other Christians, and to address the failings of the Catholic Church. Certain elements of Catholic uniformity and centralism were relaxed. Most noticeable – and controversial – of all was the abandonment in many countries of the Latin service, in favor of vernacular liturgy. With that change has also come a new readiness to adopt modern, even "pop" forms – the use of guitars and worship songs instead of formal hymns, the "folk Mass," and so on.

The Catholic Church has not been without difficulties of its own. It has faced a worsening shortage of clergy in countries of the West. Many allege that this is particularly due to its insistence on clerical celibacy. But that can only be part of the story. Many of the older, mainstream Protestant denominations do have married clergy, but have also faced the problem of declining ministerial numbers. Perhaps the rule of clerical celibacy merely serves to highlight a deeper problem, which is the growing gap between the values and expectations of the churches in the West, and the lifestyles of the population as a whole. For Catholics, this is perhaps most sharply evident in the contrast between some of the moral teachings of the Church, and popular culture. When Paul VI published Humane Vitae ("Of human life") in 1968, condemning artificial means of contraception, there were many in the Catholic Church who feared that this risked making the Church look ridiculous. The concern behind the teaching was clearly to resist the cheapening of conception, and of human life as a whole, that the emerging culture of sexual fulfillment in the West seemed to imply. It was reinforced by the Church's consistent opposition to abortion. But events have borne out some of the critics' predictions. The birth rate has dipped dramatically in America and Europe over the last thirty or forty years, and nowhere more so than in those countries that formerly could claim to be most loyally Catholic. Now, among countries with the lowest birth rate in Europe, for example, are Italy and Spain. Many young couples, even as some continue to claim to be faithful churchgoers, are simply ignoring the teaching of the Church.

Another difficulty for the Catholic Church has been the recent spate of scandals associated with child abuse. Here, too, it must be said that it is not alone. Other Christian churches – along with secular organizations, of course – have been found guilty of condoning, or at least failing to prevent, the misuse of children in their care. But the self-conscious separatism that to some extent marked Catholic culture in Britain and America until recently may have made things worse for the Church. Certainly, the intensity of the Church's commitment to maintaining Catholic schools, often run by celibate orders, and to children's homes and even adoption agencies, has put it in a particularly exposed position. At the time of writing, it is too early to say whether or not lasting damage has been done to the Church's mission in the West.

But it would be a mistake to suggest that the Catholic Church had somehow failed to adapt to the modern world. Just as, in the nineteenth century, missionary orders were able to use new forms of musical expression, and new opportunities for mass meetings, for their own purposes, so in the twentieth century, the Catholic Church has also shown itself capable of seizing the chances presented by the new mass media. A new kind of church leader, comfortable with radio and television, and able thereby to achieve something like national influence, has come into being. In America, perhaps the best-known example was Fulton J. Sheen (1895–1979), auxiliary bishop in New York and delegate to Vatican II. Sheen was one of the first church leaders in America to see the potential of television for bringing the Christian faith to a wide audience, fronting a remarkably popular weekly series, "Life is Worth Living" in the 1950s. A consummate communicator, comfortable in front of the camera, Sheen displayed a revivalist's grasp of the importance of using down-to-earth language to project saving truth. In Britain, a comparable figure would perhaps be Basil Hume (1923–99), Cardinal Archbishop of Westminster from 1976 until his death. While hardly seeking a high media profile, Hume's evident goodness and good sense, along with a certain quiet charisma, made him particularly appreciated as a public figure and leader of the Catholic Church in England. The folk Mass, and with it the readiness of Catholic musicians to adapt pop music to religious purposes, are another sign that the Church is not merely stuck in a time-warp.

Overall, the religious scene at the beginning of the twenty-first century on both sides of the Atlantic is vastly different from that of a century before. Gone, mostly, is the intense sectarian rivalry that formerly marked relations between Catholics and Protestants. Where it remains, as in Northern Ireland, it seems all the more strident and peculiar to those outside the province. Particularly after Vatican II, Catholic participation in the worldwide movement for Christian unity (the "ecumenical" movement) has marked a new spirit of mutual appreciation. Catholics, like many members of the mainstream Protestant denominations, remain anxious about the future, concerned that the shortage of clergy, and declining numbers of churchgoers in the West, indicate an increasing marginalization of the Church in western society. Yet the Church remains open to new currents of religious feeling – to charismatic expression, to new approaches to spirituality, to new forms of religious music, among other things – and that is at least a mark of its readiness to undergo renewal. As for many of the Protestant churches, whether that can be done without more thoroughgoing institutional change remains to be seen.

1 Quoted in D. H. McLeod, *Religion and the People of Western Europe 1789–1970* (Oxford University Press, 1981), p. 82.

2 J. P. Dolan, *Catholic Revivalism. The American Experience 1830–1900* (University of Notre Dame Press, 1978), p. 38.

3 J. Bossy, *The English Catholic Community 1570–1850* (DLT, London, 1975), p. 185.

4 R. Harris, Lourdes. *Body and Spirit in the Secular Age* (Allen Lane, London, 1999), p. 7.

Chapter 6

The Transformation of Traditional Worship

SO FAR IN this book we have looked at events – the story of the rise of Evangelical or revivalist religion in America and Britain, and the Catholic response. Before we turn to look at the modern missionary movement, and at the third "wave" of renewal, Pentecostalism, it is time briefly to turn aside to consider the changing ways in which Christians have worshipped over the centuries. Almost the first thing that comes to mind today, when different groups of Christians encounter one another, is the great difference in church buildings and in the styles of worship that take place within them. Sometimes Christians are surprised to find many underlying similarities. Sometimes, however, they are bewildered by the differences. Many of these differences can be traced back to specific movements in Christian history. Revivalism in particular created new forms of worship. As it sought to transform church life, it used worship as the vehicle for its distinctive message. The great variety of Christian worship today is the legacy of Christianity's history, and revivalism has been a central element of that in modern times.

Changing fashion has certainly had an influence on changing styles of worship and church architecture. But above all, changes have come about because of changing beliefs – what the specialists call "theology." For all that, at the heart of Christian history, there is a common faith in one Savior, Jesus Christ, revealed to us in the sacred witness of the Bible. As we have seen, Christians have differed considerably over how to interpret that faith, and over how to read the Scriptures. Their church buildings have been an indication of their theology. So too has the way in which they worshipped. By looking carefully at the character of different forms of worship, and at different church buildings, we can begin to understand something of the underlying structures of ideas, the theology of different communities of Christians.

This is not to say that all worship today can be explained only as the outcome of historical developments in belief. Many Christians of similar belief value different kinds of worship. The link between belief and practice is sometimes not all that direct. Sometimes similar practices can be supported by different beliefs. Within particular church traditions, there are often significant divisions over practice. In most churches in the West, for example, there is a difference between what younger people prefer as a practice of worship, and what older people tend to value. To the generational gap, we can add regional differences, and even (sometimes) ethnic and cultural differences. So this is a complex aspect of our subject, and we can only touch on it briefly here.

Christ Church, Spitalfields

Worship and the Word

By the beginning of the eighteenth century, the dominant fashion for church building among the Protestant churches of Britain and America was classical in inspiration. Buildings were square or rectangular, with rounded or square windows, and often a classical portico at the West end, with columns, where the entrance was usually located. Churches could look imposing, if large and well decorated, or homely, if small and simple. The more wealthy and prestigious churches echoed the grandiose pretensions of their builders. They made a statement about the power and significance of the faith of those who worshipped there. They stood out from their surroundings, proclaiming the social force of religion. They might be built of expensive stone, or brick, and decorated with marble inside. Humbler buildings often echoed, instead, the materials of the homes of their members, including wood as well as brick. Painted glass was a luxury rarely afforded. On both sides of the Atlantic Ocean, the same factors came into play. Wealthier, more socially aspirant Christian communities tended to build more impressive buildings. But the underlying functions were the same nevertheless. Churches needed a bell to summon people (at a time when few had watches or clocks) to worship – and a bell needs a tower or spire. In classical buildings, usually the tower was small and in the middle of the West front of the church. Churches needed wide or multiple entrances to let people in and out quickly, and windows to give natural light.

Both the similarities and the differences can be seen in church buildings of this period readily enough. Take the immense Christ Church, Spitalfields, in London, designed by Nicholas Hawksmoor (1661–1736), one-time pupil of Sir Christopher Wren. Part of an ambitious church-building scheme, the church was erected between 1714 and 1729 to serve the population on the fringes of the City of London. Its scale and design are dramatic. To an almost square ground layout for the main part of the church, Hawksmoor added a Tuscan West porch and a three-stage tower. The church had a full peal of eight bells from 1730, enlarged to ten later in the century. Inside the church, to maximize accommodation, Hawksmoor placed galleries around North, East, and West sides of the church. Christ Church is grand, overpowering, and sumptuous. Yet its overall conception is not dissimilar from that of much more humble buildings of the period. St Mary's, Battersea, London, built in the 1770s, is a more modest instance. It looks to all intents and purposes like an American colonial church. In colonial America itself, there were numerous wooden examples, many of which were replaced by more permanent buildings in the nineteenth century. The Old West Church in Calais, Vermont is perhaps a surviving case in point. Built in 1825, in fact it was essentially a copy of the meeting houses built a century earlier in New England. In an arrangement virtually unknown in Britain, the church served several denominations at once. It did not have a separate West porch, unlike many New England churches, and it was built partly of wood, but its overall design echoed that of Christ Church, Spitalfields – a rectangular building, holding ground floor box pews, with galleries on three sides, and a small spire at the West end of the church.

From a grandiose Episcopal church in the Old World to a humble community church in the New, styles of church architecture for much of the eighteenth and early nineteenth centuries were similar, then. Why was this so? Quite simply, in all cases here the design reflected the supreme importance given in pre-nineteenth century Protestantism to the preaching of the Word as the highpoint of worship. All these churches shared something in common with the theatres of the time. They gave particular prominence to the leading performer, the minister or priest, who would lead worship, read the Bible aloud, and above all expound the Word of God to his congregation. That is why pulpits or reading desks were usually placed prominently in the East end of the church, and seating – either on the ground floor, or in the galleries arranged on the remaining three sides around the preacher. Buildings were relatively squat – not long and elongated, as in many medieval buildings – so that the hearers were always within earshot of the preacher. Ceilings were usually square, and relatively low, in order to maximize the sound of the sermon. Even in Britain where, outside the largest cities, very few new churches were built before the end of the eighteenth century, ancient medieval churches were adapted to suit this purpose by blocking up the chancel or choir (the large space at the East end where in the Middle Ages the choir would sit, and where the Mass used to be said), by putting in galleries, and by replacing the open seating with box pews. Changing fashion in the nineteenth century ensured that most of these alterations were themselves taken out again. But here and there, examples survive. One of the most striking is that of St Mary's, Whitby, where the box pews and galleries crowd around the high pulpit still.

St. Mary's, Whitby

Now what is obvious straightaway to any visitor to these churches today is that the worship for which they were designed would have been a static affair. This was especially because pews were often rented out to particular families. The congregation would assemble, and expect to stay put for most, if not all, of the service. There were no processions, and little congregational movement. In Anglican and Episcopal churches, the service would have been from the Book of Common Prayer. Only rarely would it have been a communion service. In the countryside, there might not have been more than three or four communion services a year. That figure would have risen to one a month in the towns. Other denominations, particularly in America, would use their own order of service – usually much less fixed in content than was the case for Anglicans. The minister would lead the congregation in reading prayers, in Scripture reading, and in the sermon. Sermons in all cases were usually long – often above an hour. For a dedicated minister, preparation of the weekly sermon would have been one of his most important tasks. For the congregation, the sermon was often the moment when the religion the minister represented was translated into a wholesome, improving message.

In almost all these churches, music was important, too. But it was not church music as is familiar to us now. There were few choirs, and few organs. In some churches, there were "church bands" – a small group of instrumentalists, perhaps including a violinist, a flautist, and one or two brass players – that accompanied the singing. But mostly the singing was congregational, and unaccompanied. Psalms were sung, but in a metrical, rhyming form more like the hymns we know today. The most famous collection of psalm settings by the middle of the eighteenth century in English-speaking countries was probably that of Nahum Tate and Nicholas Brady, introduced in 1696, though the Scottish Psalter of 1650 was also popular. The practice of "lining out" was common: a clerk would sing one line at a time, followed by the congregation. Hymns began to be introduced into worship in the course of the eighteenth century. It was particularly the "free churches" of Britain and America that pioneered their use. American hymn-singing became popular during the Great Awakening. One of the leading early American hymn-writers was Samuel Davies (1723–61), a Presbyterian minister who took up an itinerant ministry after the traumatic death of his family in 1747. One of his best-known hymns today is a magnificent ode to God's majesty:

> Great God of wonders, all thy ways
> are matchless, God-like and divine;
> but the fair glories of thy grace
> more God-like and unrivalled shine:
> who is a pardoning God like thee,
> or who has grace so rich and free?

The Methodist movement in Britain and America also popularized the practice of hymn-singing. Charles Wesley, perhaps the most famous hymn-writer of all, wrote over 6,000. Many are still sung today, and include favorites such "Lo, he comes with clouds descending," "Hark! The herald angels sing," "Love's redeeming work is done," and this great revival barnstormer:

> And can it be that I should gain
> an interest in the Savior's blood?
> Died he for me, who caused his pain?
> For me, who him to death pursued?
> Amazing love! How can it be
> that thou, my God, shouldst die for me?

The great advantage of hymns was that they could present teaching in an accessible form. With a catchy tune, they could be learnt easily. They lent themselves to use by large gatherings of people, perhaps led from the front by a minister or a musician. Summing up the experiences and emotions of people, they could help to prepare them for the saving message of the sermon, or they could express gratitude for the experience of God's grace that flowed from accepting the proclamation of the gospel.

The increasing adoption of hymn-singing, however, marked the changing spirit of worship. Under the influence of revivalism, a new yearning for intense spiritual experience was finding its way into the formerly sober ethos of Protestant worship. Large revivalist meetings – especially if held in the open air – could not be galvanized by metrical psalms. They needed memorable, repeated tunes that could be used with words often learnt off by heart. Hymn-singing would work an assembly into a fever of anticipation, so that the word preached by the worship leader could bring his or her hearers to an intense conviction of their need for repentance and conversion. Hymn-singing then could reinforce their new-found confidence in Christ. Gradually, the practice of hymn-singing spread to the more traditional, well-established denominations. It was adopted widely in Anglican and Episcopal churches by the middle of the nineteenth century. New hymns and worship songs were introduced constantly. The modern worship chorus, and the use of guitars and drums to accompany popular music in church, is no more than an updated version of this revivalist practice. In their own day, the great hymn-writers were every bit as contemporary as are the songwriters of today.

Revivalism, expressed through Evangelical belief, changed profoundly the feel of Protestant worship. Of course, it remained the case that, in the traditional churches, a much less fluid style of worship was dominant. The use of printed prayer books, in an ordered spirit, were characteristic of much of Protestantism throughout the nineteenth and twentieth centuries. Indeed, even in those religious traditions in which the revivalist spirit flourished, such as Methodism, there was an inbuilt tendency for the informal, spontaneous, and ecstatic gradually to give way to the ordered, and predictable. That was part of the cycle of consolidation and renewal we have noted throughout Christian history. Large, open-air meetings were one thing. People could be assembled and inspired by charismatic preachers, and by the outpouring of music and praise. But how could they build a permanent religious community? How could they harness popular enthusiasm, and turn it into something that could be transmitted from one generation to the next? That was the difficulty Protestants faced. Almost invariably the great, spontaneous open-air gatherings would in time come to be replaced by the construction of permanent church buildings, with open-air meetings taking place occasionally on a predictable, organized basis. Along with permanence and stability came, often, affluence too. The very success of the values engendered by conversion and the pursuit of Christian perfection could lead to a more responsible attitude to money and employment, and the gradual accumulation of wealth. No one could have put it better than John Wesley himself:

> I do not see how it is possible, in the nature of things, for any revival of true religion to continue long. For religion must necessarily produce both industry and frugality, and these cannot but produce riches. But as riches increase, so will pride, anger, and love of the world in all its branches. How then is it possible that Methodism, that is, a religion of the heart, though it flourishes now as a green bay tree, should continue in this state? For the Methodists in every place grow diligent and frugal; consequently they increase in goods. Hence they proportionately increase in pride, in anger, in the desire of the flesh, the desire of the eyes, and the pride of life. So, although the form of

religion remains, the spirit is swiftly vanishing away. Is there no way to prevent this – this continual decay of pure religion?[1]

Wesley's words were aimed at the growing social respectability of Methodists, but much of what he said was also true of the constant tendency of spontaneous revival to embed itself in ordered, permanent communities of believers. Methodism led to the creation of new denominations, and the building of new churches. These churches looked, to all intents and purposes, much like those of other Protestants.

Catholicism and the Church triumphant

Ironically, for much of the eighteenth and early nineteenth centuries, Catholic church building also followed the same basic classical program as that of Protestantism. New Catholic churches of this period were also often rectangular, almost square in shape, with a classical façade at the West end. The "Baroque" style, fashionable across Europe in the late seventeenth and early eighteenth centuries, could also lend itself, however, to a flamboyance that was not generally encountered in the Protestant churches of the same period in Britain and America – with the exception of some of the London churches. The Baroque Jesuit Church of Lucerne, built in the 1660s at the edge of the lake, is a good example of this more ornamental fashion. It too is a simple rectangle, yet its West front and two domed towers carry much decoration.

These Baroque Catholic churches served a different liturgical purpose from their Protestant counterparts. Their focal point inside was the high altar at the East end of the church, often a highly elaborate marble or stone affair, surrounded again by ornate decoration. This asserted the central role of the Mass in Catholic worship. Under the influence of the Catholic Counter-Reformation, the Mass was re-emphasized by bringing its celebration publicly to the fore. Gone were the screens that had obscured the sanctuaries of medieval churches. The exaltation of the altar

The baroque Jesuit Church of Lucerne

in Baroque churches symbolized the elevated significance of the Mass, but it also presented the Mass as a public spectacle. In so doing, it drove home the point that all the people participated in the sacrifice of the Mass. It was, in a sense, liturgy as show, but never less than utterly in earnest for all that. Yet the arrangement of these Baroque churches also shared something in common with Protestant churches. For, again under the influence of the Counter-Reformation, preaching was also stressed. The faithful were to be re-educated in the doctrines of the faith, so that the misunderstandings and (as Catholics saw it) the erroneous teachings of the Reformation would never again have the chance of drawing them away. Pulpits were prominent in these churches, too.

Baroque showiness was the perfect vehicle for the sense of the Church triumphant that marked Catholic experience of the second half of the seventeenth century and persisted into the eighteenth. The Catholic Church had survived Europe's religious conflicts, and picked itself up from the blows of the

Reformation. The papacy might be in difficulties, but, until the French Revolution, no one seriously suspected that the very existence of the Church might be in doubt. This sense of confidence was never lost altogether, even when translated into the situation of North America. Catholicism was of course well rooted in those parts of America ceded by or won by conquest from Mexico, Spain, and France in the early nineteenth century. Here one would find Baroque churches, too, though sometimes bewilderingly florid in their decoration – a sign of adaptation to local culture. But in the building of new churches in the United States and in Canada, the classical, Baroque conventions continued to apply. The oldest Catholic cathedral in America, the Basilica of the Assumption in Baltimore is an excellent example of this. Built from 1806 to 1818, this is monumental classicism, often described as the masterpiece of its architect, Benjamin Henry Latrobe (1764–1820), who also designed the Capitol. The basilica combines the practicality of rectangular form with the grandeur of a central dome, not altogether unlike St Paul's, London, though its inspiration is Greek rather than Roman. Another example is Cincinnati Cathedral, dedicated to "St Peter in Chains." Built from 1841 to 1845, this was also evidently influenced by classical Greek architecture, with a pillared West portico.

The return of medievalism

No sooner was the cement dry on Cincinnati Cathedral, however, than a quite different religious ethos was beginning to gain ground. The Gothic style, with its tall, narrow buildings and its pointed arches, had died a long, lingering death in Europe. In England, though the Reformation had brought to a halt the massive wave of church rebuilding that had been underway since the fifteenth century, even into the seventeenth century here and there, on occasions, small local churches were often built in the Gothic style. Perhaps local builders simply did not know any other way of doing it. Even the great Baroque architects occasionally dabbled in Gothic – usually when restoring or completing existing ancient buildings. Hawksmoor's towers at Westminster Abbey are a good example, added as late as the 1720s and 1730s. Then, also in the eighteenth century, a few wealthy people began to dabble in the Gothic style for their country houses. This was part of a deliberate cultivation of the mysterious and exotic mood that they thought the medieval style had expressed. It was a flight from the more ordered forms of classicism, a reaction perhaps against the easy optimism of much of the century's "enlightened" thought. It was a rich man's indulgence. But it expressed, nevertheless, something more important than that. It suggested a desire to rediscover something of the perceived social and religious unity of the Middle Ages.

Such a desire went hand in hand with impulses for religious renewal reawakened by the impact of the French Revolution. We have seen these impulses at work in the Catholic Church. They were also at work within Protestantism, however. Particularly in the Anglican churches, but also within Lutheran churches, a new spirit of appreciation of medieval Christendom gradually arose. In Anglicanism, this began as the "Oxford Movement" in the 1830s, led by a small group of Oxford clergy and academics, who resisted what they saw as the rationalist spirit of the age. It became, in time, something called the "Anglo-Catholic revival," a movement to re-emphasize sacramental theology, and particularly the Eucharist or Mass, and to recover much of the ceremonial of the medieval church. Anglo-Catholicism spread to America, and to other Anglican churches throughout the world.

The new fashion for Gothic became very widespread indeed. But it was particularly encouraged by a new generation of architects and artists, who idealized the Middle Ages and sought to recreate its world of faith as a critical response to what they saw as the drabness of modern industrialism. Perhaps the most famous of all was Augustus Welby Northmore Pugin (1812–52), a convert to

Roman Catholicism who died relatively young, but not before he had revolutionized British architecture by his buildings and by his proclamation of his ideals in a series of publications. Pugin's medievalism was apparent in his conviction that the Middle Ages were the summit of human religious and artistic creativity. In a series of publications, he roundly condemned the classical style, and functionalism, of buildings of his day, and advocated the use of Gothic. The most famous of these was a book whose title has to be retained in full to grasp the thrust of Pugin's argument: *Contrasts, A Parallel between the Noble Edifices of the 14th and 15th centuries and Similar buildings of the Present Day. Showing a Decay of Taste* (1836). Encouraged by Pugin and others, the rage for all things Gothic caught on remarkably quickly. By the middle of the nineteenth century it appeared to be sweeping all before it. Even railway stations, town halls, and hotels – let alone churches – were built in this style.

Some of the most splendid buildings of the nineteenth century were in the Gothic style – the Houses of Parliament in London, designed by Sir Charles Barry, and furnished and decorated inside by Pugin, is an excellent example. This was true above all of churches, however. In Britain, new cathedrals were built in the Gothic style for the first time since the Middle Ages – the Anglican cathedral at Truro, for example, designed by the architect J. L. Pearson and built from 1880 to 1910, and the Catholic cathedral at Arundel, designed by Joseph Hansom (designer of the Hansom cab), and completed in 1873. The Gothic style also caught on rapidly in America. One of the earliest American Gothic churches was St John's Episcopal Church in Savannah, completed in 1850. Perhaps the most famous American Gothic churches are cathedrals. St Patrick's Cathedral in Manhattan was begun in 1858. Work was suspended during the Civil War, resumed in 1865, and not finished until the early twentieth century. Over four hundred feet long, St Patrick's is a French Gothic cathedral in conception. The Episcopal cathedral of St John the Divine, also in New York, was begun in 1892

Truro Cathedral

St Patrick's Cathedral, New York

in an early Gothic "Romanesque" style, but when the original firm of architects collapsed in 1907, a new design was implemented to a later Gothic style, taking the length of the projected cathedral to over 600 feet. This colossal building remains unfinished even now.

These are great buildings indeed. Yet, surprisingly, Gothic was not necessarily a sign of luxury. Gothic buildings were not necessarily more expensive than classical ones. Gothic proved to be an immensely adaptable style. Brick could be used instead of stone. Brick-built buildings might be faced with stone to look to all intents and purposes like medieval buildings – a neat and economical solution to the problem of squaring taste with expense. Instead of hand-crafted fittings, mass-produced ornamentation could be used. There were even catalogues of Gothic-style church fittings, and of temporary church buildings (made in wood or corrugated iron). The new industrialism itself could supply the needs of Gothic-hungry customers.

Furthermore, the adaptability of Gothic was not just a question of materials and expense. It was also a question of theology and patterns of worship. Medievalism did particularly enhance those traditions within Christianity that valued the sacraments. Gothic architects got rid of boxed pews, and replaced them with open pews and wide aisles. Processions became possible again. The use of stained glass for windows, elaborate carved stonework, pointed arches, and spires, all fitted a view that consciously sought to emulate the faith of the Middle Ages. For all these reasons, Gothic caught on particularly with Roman Catholics, and with Catholic movements within some of the Protestant churches. And it remained popular well into the twentieth century. Britain's largest cathedral, the Anglican cathedral at Liverpool, was completed only in 1978 (work having begun in 1904), yet it was designed by Sir Giles Gilbert Scott in the Gothic style. Yet Gothic could also work in other Protestant traditions. It was relatively easy to adapt the rectangular form of classicism into the Gothic style, by use of pointed windows, spires, and such like.

Liverpool Anglican Cathedral

Such a change did not interfere with the basic function of the building. Gothic churches could serve preaching of the Word as well as could classical buildings. By the middle of the nineteenth century, Methodists, Congregationalists, Baptists, and others were beginning tentatively to experiment with Gothic. Such a change could also be read as a significant statement of confidence and self-respect. Particularly in Britain, where dissenting churches continued to feel looked down on by their established rivals, to build a church in Gothic might show that you were just as convinced of the importance of your beliefs as were the Anglicans, for example, down the road.

Thus Gothic could be adapted to suit revivalist congregations as well as more traditional worship. Yet we should remember that revivalism, by its very nature, was uncomfortable with the fixed demands that large, elaborate buildings imposed on congregations. Perhaps a good illustration of this is the Salvation Army. Founded in London in the late 1860s as the "Christian Mission" by William and Catherine Booth, this was a deliberate attempt to bring the light of the gospel to the poorest levels of society. It spread rapidly to America. The Salvation Army, as it came to be called in the early 1880s, broke many apparent taboos. It gave great prominence to the role of women, who could preach, teach, and organize Army congregations alongside male officers. It promoted street preaching, which often attracted large crowds, some of whom might be hostile. It led street processions, too, with brass bands and chorus singing. None of these things were unique to the Army, but they were drawn together in a quite distinctive and impressively organized combination. Everything in the Army's ideals counted against the construction of elaborate, Gothic-style churches. Their mission halls, or "Citadels" as they were often called, were small, functional halls. The poverty of the Army's members was partly responsible for this. But it was also an aspect of the spirit of "traveling light." The revivalist instincts that still run through the Army today have always sat light to investment in ecclesiastical architecture.

The reaction: Modernism

In the twentieth century, church design changed again. Dramatically so. Suddenly, on both sides of the Atlantic, the financial situation of churches worsened after the First World War. In Britain, the churches were entering a very long, protracted period of consolidation and relative decline already. Many churches begun before the war were never finished. New churches were built for the expanding suburbs of London and other major cities, but the costs of building pressed on hard-up congregations more heavily than ever before. In America, by contrast, churches were entering a period of growth. Yet the Great Depression there also affected the churches. Moreover, a new spirit of disillusionment with the ideals of the nineteenth century was running through

The Unity Temple, Oak Park, Illinois, designed by Frank Lloyd Wright

society, and even through the churches. It issued in a shift in design fashion toward "Modernism." By the far the most impressive "Modernist" churches are mostly post-Second World War. In America, however, a sign of the future was laid out as early as 1905, when the pioneering modernist architect Frank Lloyd Wright (1867–1959) designed the Unity Temple at Oak Park in Illinois, a Unitarian church. Cubist in conception, and built of concrete, it looked quite unlike any other church of its age. Though Wright was a Unitarian by upbringing, and designed mostly Unitarian churches, he did show how Modernism could be used for much more traditional, "orthodox" Christian communities. His Greek Orthodox Church of the Annunciation at Wauwautosa, Wisconsin, completed in 1956, is a case in point – a circular, concrete and glass building that looks not altogether unlike a flying saucer.

In Britain, two examples stand out. One is the new Anglican cathedral at Coventry, built adjacent to the ruins of the old cathedral, burnt out in a fire-storm caused by German bombing in 1940. The new cathedral, completed in 1962 and designed by Basil Spence, is a massive departure from the practice of Victorian church building. Even more so is the Catholic cathedral of Christ the King, Liverpool. The fourth building to be attempted on the site, this is a huge concrete and colored glass corona, built in five years from 1962 to 1967 to a design by Frederick Gibberd. The modernity of the design is a striking to the late Gothic style of the Anglican cathedral nearby.

Here again it is impossible to say that Modernism suited one theological style rather than another. Nevertheless, it did perhaps rid some churches of the belief that the goal of church growth was a permanent, Gothic building. Modern revivalist churches in particular have freed themselves of that illusion. The rise of the house church movement – which we shall look at in a later chapter – reinforced this sense. Congregations could meet in cinemas, or in school halls, or in village halls, or even in halls belonging to other churches. What is important for contemporary worship –

particularly in the Evangelical or revivalist style – is a large space for people to meet, and power points to run the electronic musical instruments, microphones and projectors on which they thrive. It does not particularly matter if the building is impressive and visible from outside or not – nowadays, churches can advertise where they can be found through television, radio, the local newspapers, and the Internet. All of this suggests a very different function for a building from the requirements of previous generations. The Vineyard church in Cincinnati is a striking example of this. A church community of thousands, which has moved several times since its formation in the early 1960s, it now occupies a site of several acres, with a large church, offices, and nursery and social facilities. Its style of worship is easy, popular, and accessible, and it is backed up by a formidable collection of electronic equipment. It advertises itself through a sophisticated website updated continually, and has mastered the exploitation of modern technology to execute an evangelistic ministry not in principle so very different from the ministry of the old-style revivalist preachers.

1 Cited in R. Southey, *Life of Wesley* (Frederick Warne & Co, London, new ed., 1889), p. 516.

Chapter 7

A Mission to Convert the World

THE RISE OF revivalism in the modern world is the story of a restless desire to extend the mission of the gospel. Revivalists sought to make converts, whether from those who were nominal Christians, but lacking in conviction, or from those who had never professed the Christian faith before. By its very nature, their work was missionary. Yet they often made a practical distinction between mission to their own kind, and mission to non-Christian peoples in other territories or countries. The former might be called "home" or "domestic" mission, and the latter "overseas" mission. In Britain, this distinction was very clear. Since its people had long ago been converted at least to nominal Christianity, the task of the evangelist was to rekindle the flame of true religion in their hearts. From the perspective of Britain, all mission to non-Christian peoples was "overseas" mission. This did not mean, however,

Missionary preaching to the Indians

that British Evangelicals were complacent about the real state of belief in Britain. Far from it. Especially in the new industrial towns and cities, there had grown up a population that they were convinced showed all the signs of real heathenism – indifference to religion, an abundance of sin, living conditions of squalor. So they could speak of the cities as "outcast" places, or as "forgotten" or "unknown." It was significant that the Salvationist William Booth's book advocating a scheme of social as well as religious renewal should be called *In Darkest England and the Way Out* (1890).

William Booth

In America, the same sharp distinction between home and overseas mission could not be sustained until the twentieth century. For American evangelists before then, the most obvious and immediate missionary field was the expanding frontier, a place that confusingly overlapped internal and external, outsiders and insiders. It was a place of ever newly founded settlements, of expanding communities of migrants, of "heathen" native Americans and unregenerate settlers. It was the context in which the expansion of American revivalism really took place. But that did not mean that American Protestants were indifferent to the needs of mission "overseas." They too were to sponsor a great wave of western missionary effort in other parts of the world.

Yet the difference between the American and British contexts points to a fact that we must at least acknowledge. For all that the aims of missionaries were to convert the non-Christian peoples of the world to the Christian faith, and so to extend the realm of Christ's religion, their activity could not but be affected by, and bound up with, the political and economic ambitions of their sending countries. In the British case, this meant the rise of its overseas Empire, and its eventual liquidation into the Commonwealth. In the case of America, this meant the growth of the nation itself throughout the nineteenth century. "Overseas" American expansion was limited. Having escaped from the British Empire, Americans were naturally reluctant to join in the imperial pretensions of the Old World powers. Yet, in the twentieth century, wars begun in the Old World drew in America, and ushered in, eventually, a period of American economic and political supremacy that is still with us.

All of this means that the story of the Protestant mission to the world is a complex one – a substantial subject in its own right, for which there is no space here to do more than indicate the barest of outlines. Our purpose is simply to show how the experience of revivalism in America and Britain also had another side, a readiness to carry the same spiritual conviction and evangelical fervor to other peoples than those who lived on either side of the Atlantic.

Evangelicalism and Empire

The problem of overseas mission was present to the British churches from the very beginning of British colonial expansion. As we saw in Chapter 3, the foundation of the Society for the Propagation of Christian Knowledge (SPCK) in 1698, and the Society for the Propagation of the Gospel (SPG) in 1701, was a sign of this. The one concentrated on the founding of schools and the publication of Bibles and tracts for distribution overseas, the other on providing for the spiritual welfare of British people overseas, and on evangelizing non-Christian people. The efforts of these two societies were coordinated, and concentrated on America and the Caribbean for much of the eighteenth century. Later in the century, as British territorial expansion continued in India, and then began in Africa, the SPG in particular extended its operations to include these new colonies.

By then, however, other impulses were also coming to the fore. Under the influence of Anglican Evangelicalism, the Church Missionary Society (CMS) was founded as a result of some disillusionment with the older Anglican societies. CMS had as its first secretary Thomas Scott, the famous Evangelical biblical commentator, and it pioneered missionary work in Africa, the Middle East, and the Far East. This was merely symptomatic, however, of a general Evangelical concern for overseas mission. CMS in fact was anticipated by the formation of a Baptist Mission Society (BMS) in 1792, and by the predominantly Congregationalist London Missionary Society (LMS) in 1795, and followed by the non-denominational British and Foreign Bible Society (the "Bible Society") in 1804. One of the most famous of the early missionaries was the Baptist William Carey (1761–1834), who arrived in India in 1793, and began intensive missionary work. Carey translated the Bible into Bengali, and visited and evangelized in Bengal, until his appointment to the new Fort William College in Calcutta in 1801.

American societies also were formed in this period. The American Board for Foreign Missions (ABFM) was formed in 1810, partly through the agency of Lyman Beecher (1775–1863), one of the great Presbyterian revivalist preachers of his day. Beecher was also influential in the founding of the American Bible Society in 1816, the Colonization Society for liberated slaves in 1817, and the American Home Missionary Society. The ABFM worked fast, and was sending its first missionaries overseas to India and the Far East by 1812. Among its earliest missionaries was Adoniram Judson (1788–1850), who worked as a missionary in Burma for forty years, and married four times and was widowed three times. Stories of the Judsons' heroic labors, says one modern historian, "were best-sellers in antebellum America, indicating that confidence in the spread

Lyman Beecher and his family

of the faith in America was broadening to include eager anticipation of its spread elsewhere."[1] Other societies also came into being, such as the General Missionary Convention of the Baptist Denomination in the United States for Missions in 1814. This was a sign of the growing strength of the Baptists during the "Second Great Awakening." Despite great efforts to support overseas mission, however, the complications of the American situation were illustrated by the comparable efforts poured into "home" mission in the same period, and into halting attempts to evangelize the Native American peoples.

The formation of the missionary societies set the scene for the great age of American and European missionary endeavor in the second half of the nineteenth century. So extensive was the work of the societies in this period, that nothing more than a selection of events and personalities can be highlighted. Much of the exploration of equatorial Africa was undertaken by missionaries – perhaps the best known of them being David Livingstone (1813–73). American missionary societies helped to open up Japan to the West, Catholic missions having been brought to a

During the nineteenth century the population of America expanded rapidly

bloody end in the sixteenth and seventeenth centuries. Episcopalians, Presbyterians, Reformed, and Baptists all entered the country in the 1860s and began work there. China too experienced intense missionary activity in the second half of the nineteenth century. After the American–Spanish war of 1898, the Philippines came under American domination, enabling the entry into the islands of Presbyterian, Baptist, and Methodist missionaries. American Protestant missionaries also entered India, working alongside the British mission societies. West Africa was particularly targeted by CMS, and it was in Nigeria that the first ever non-white Anglican bishop was appointed, Samuel Adjai Crowther (1807–89). A freed slave, Crowther (or "Ajayi" to give him his original name) worked mainly in East Nigeria after his consecration in Canterbury Cathedral.

By the end of the nineteenth century, thousands of missionaries had been sent from Britain and America to the four corners of the earth. In Africa and the Far East, the foundations had been laid for the stupendous growth of the Christian faith that was to occur later in the twentieth century. British imperialism, and American affluence, between them had provided an umbrella for a massive expansion of the English-speaking churches. It seemed, on the brink of the First World War, that it really was possible to speak of the ambition of proclaiming Christ to the whole world. In the words of the great John R. Mott (1865–1955), the American missionary and leader of the Student Volunteer Movement, it was possible to conceive of "the evangelization of the world in this generation."[2] In 1910 a combined World Missionary Conference was held in Edinburgh. Drawing more than 1,200 representatives from all over the world, but particularly from Britain and America, and chaired by Mott, the conference sought to commit itself to raising almost an army of missionary volunteers. Such had been the advances in the preceding half-century, that it must have looked to all present that Christianity really was on the verge of becoming the great world religion.

Imposition and adaptation

What was the Christianity of the missionaries really like, however? In reality it was not essentially different from that of the sending churches themselves. Its basic form was Evangelical in the main, as Evangelicalism had captured most of the main Protestant denominations in America and Britain by the second half of the nineteenth century. A few missionary societies reflected a different spirit. Two British societies – the SPG, and the Universities' Mission to Central Africa (UMCA) – carried a High Church, or even "Anglo-Catholic" spirit. But their impact, along with that of comparable American associations, was relatively limited, and certainly concentrated only in a few parts of the world, such as South and East Africa. The Evangelical theology of most of the major missionary societies was to facilitate cooperation between them in the early twentieth century. It also enabled something of the methods and the spirit of revivalism to emerge eventually in the mission field.

This last point was slow to develop, however, as missionaries faced the obvious barriers of language and culture. The first task of missionaries was usually one of translation and learning. They had to learn the languages of the people among whom they were to work, as experience quickly showed that relying on interpreters was counter-productive. They also had to learn something of the cultural context in which they were to work, since their teaching and preaching would be of no avail if they could not relate it to the particular situations of the people whom they were evangelizing. A moment's reflection bears out the obviousness of this point. To a people who, for example, might have no experience of fishing, the gospel stories and parables about fishing and fishermen might seem nonsensical. A hunter-gatherer people, who did not keep sheep or cattle, likewise might have no understanding of the parables about the good shepherd. Great care had to be taken in translating the Scriptures into native languages, accordingly, and the missionary societies built up a great deal of expertise in the skills of language learning and translation. With all these potential hindrances, the work of a missionary in, for example, Africa, or in India, could not possibly proceed as it might have done in America or in Britain. The organized, revivalist techniques of large, open meetings, hymn-singing, preaching to carry a congregation to a pitch of anxiety about sin and judgment, and the calling forward of the penitent and those waiting to receive Jesus, could not function in the mission field until something like a preliminary task of teaching and preparation had been carried out. Evangelicalism might inspire missionaries to go overseas, but the conventional techniques of revival had to be a second stage of the missionary task.

Moreover, in time it became clear that the difficulties facing the missionaries were not simply those of translation and learning. Unless missionaries were prepared to go very far indeed in adapting their methods and forms of teaching to the cultures they encountered, there was a serious risk their work would simply appear as one more form of western domination. Western religion was, so it seemed, being imposed upon native cultures across the world. Missionaries often seemed blithely unaware that their religious convictions had taken shape in the particular conditions of western culture and society, and could not always be translated with ease into the values and cultures of the mission field. Indeed, the mission field could raise serious theological and ethical questions for the missionaries. One instance was that of the practice of polygamy in some cultures. It was one thing to condemn it from the Christian perspective. But what then could be done about wives who were seemingly to be cast out from their husbands' homes? How should the role of women in this context be redefined? Another instance centered on the renegade English bishop in South Africa, J. W. Colenso (1814–83). Widely condemned for his questioning of the historical authenticity of the Pentateuch, the first five books of the Bible, Colenso was also a pioneering voice in the extensive adaptation of Christianity to the Zulu context in which he worked. Not only did Colenso refuse to force the wives of polygamists to be divorced on their baptism, but he also differed substantially from other missionaries in his readiness to research the Zulus' own concepts of God and the

J. W. Colenso (Illustration © Topfoto)

spirits and to use these as ways of articulating the Christian faith for the Zulu people.

Colenso's efforts drew down upon him criticism from many of his contemporaries, who feared that his experiments with translation compromised the truth of Christianity as they knew it. But Colenso – for all his controversy as a biblical interpreter – was simply one who grasped early on that Christianity could not possibly stand a chance of attracting followers in the mission field on any sizeable scale unless it could be detached from the imperial or western context of its sending churches. In the modern jargon, the Christian faith had to be "inculturated" in the mission field – that is, it had to be adapted in its forms of expression to make sense to the peoples to whom it was being brought. In this process, the Christianity of the missionaries would subtly change. Many of the features of churchgoing that the missionaries had brought with them in time would change or disappear – the hymn-singing, the putting on special dress for church, and so on. Christianity might become "Africanized," for example. At that point, paradoxically, many of the more explosive features of Western revivalism also surfaced – the spontaneity, the emotional intensity, the experience of outpourings of special gifts of the spirit, long, ecstatic meetings, and so on.

Thus, the Christianity that has emerged as an authentic, "native" movement in countries formerly evangelized by missionaries from the West has rejected many of the specific cultural forms of the nineteenth century, but it has developed similarities to the more chaotic and ecstatic revivalism of an earlier period. As these Christian churches continue to expand dramatically in Africa, in the Far East, and even in South America, they present an aspect of Christian experience that is strangely familiar. It is an aspect also encountered directly in the West itself, in the third great wave of revival to which we must now briefly turn – the Pentecostal, or charismatic, revival.

1 Noll, A *History of Christianity in the United States and Canada*, p. 187.

2 K. Clements, *Faith on the Frontier. A Life of J. H. Oldham* (T & T Clark, Edinburgh, 1999), p. 65.

Chapter 8

THE PENTECOSTAL REVIVAL

THROUGHOUT THIS BOOK, we have been looking at the waves of renewal that have run through the Christian Church in the West in the modern period. We have seen that, before the twentieth century, these could be described roughly as two, the Evangelical revival (or "Awakening"), which transformed Protestantism from the early eighteenth century, and the Catholic revival, which began to gather momentum in the early nineteenth century. Nothing is very neat or tidy about the language we have used to describe these events. We have used the terms "Evangelical" and "revivalist" almost interchangeably at times. "Revivalism" could describe a particular set of practices and beliefs, including mass meetings, the encouragement of conversions, and a theology of the conviction of sin and need for repentance. In that sense, it could be taken to mean something distinct within Evangelical Protestantism. Not all Evangelicals were "revivalists." On the other hand, mass revivalism did affect virtually the whole body of the Protestant denominations, and led to the creation of something like a common Evangelical culture. It is not easy to draw a sharp distinction between Evangelicalism and revivalism. Moreover, "revivalism" could be applied more widely still. We have seen how there was a Catholic revivalism. It had ts own distinct methods, and yet it also owed something to its rival movement in Protestantism. And yet even certain Protestant denominations experienced omething like a "Catholic revival" – a renewal of sacramental theology – in the ourse of the nineteenth century. There may be somewhat confusing overlaps etween these terms, then, but it does seem to answer best the complexity of the istorical evidence to use them in this deliberately blurred way.

As we shall see in this chapter, the terminology is further complicated by events n the twentieth century. Yet, before we touch on those, we should at least point out hat, for all that they had their origins in historical crises and changes in Protestantism nd Catholicism centuries ago, the impact of these two great waves of renewal is still very much with us. The Catholic Church still uses many of the same methods of the great age of Catholic revivalism, and is recognizably the same church. Arguably, Protestantism today in most of its manifestations is evidently the heir of the Evangelical revival. Indeed, even "revivalism" in its more narrow form has continued to shape much of Protestant life and thought. Throughout the twentieth century, there have been great revivalist preachers who have fitted the picture we have described of figures like John Wesley and Dwight Moody. Early in the twentieth century, Billy Sunday (1862–1935) was one such. A former baseball player, Sunday was converted in 1886, and later ordained into the Presbyterian ministry. His colorful preaching style, deploying the arts of mimicry and anecdote, won him a wide following, with much newspaper coverage. Sunday – characteristically for his period – was a strong supporter of the temperance movement. In the middle of the century, the great modern evangelist Billy Graham (born in 1918) came into prominence. Raised in North Carolina, Graham became known as a traveling preacher when he worked for Youth for Christ in the 1940s and 1950s. Backed by the publisher William Randolph Hearst, Graham's summer crusade of 1949 became a sensational success, drawing thousands into the tent he had pitched

Billy Sunday

in Los Angeles. In a move that provoked some criticism at the time, however, Graham deliberately sought to work alongside Christian churches of many different opinions. His "ecumenical" instincts have even extended to cooperation with Roman Catholics, a development inconceivable a century before. His tours of Britain in the 1950s and 1960s were also immensely successful, and there is no comparable British figure of the late twentieth century to match him. His charismatic personality and evident success gained him entry to the White House, and a succession of presidents from Harry Truman on have invited him there. In Graham, modern Protestant revivalism has attained more than a measure of respectability.

Dr Billy Graham – has been described as America's spiritual counselor (Photograph © Topfoto)

Born more than ten years later than Graham, Martin Luther King, Jr (1929–68) has achieved mythic status in modern America. But King, like Billy Graham, in essence represented a revivalist, Evangelical tradition that has worked its way thoroughly into the mainstream of modern American Christianity. Himself the son of a Baptist pastor, King became pastor of the Dexter Avenue Baptist Church in Montgomery, Alabama. It

"I have a dream"
– Rev Martin Luther King, Jr

was the civil rights movement that brought him to national prominence, partly through his organization of the Southern Christian Leadership Conference (SCLC). Though it drew support in so many ways from the black churches, the history of the civil rights movement touches on many aspects of American life that lie strictly beyond our narrative here. Yet the leadership of the SCLC contained a preponderance of black pastors, and the speaking style of King and others echoed exactly the revivalist rhetoric and passion of Evangelical church leaders over the centuries. Moreover, King's conception of civil rights, and his advocacy of them, arose directly from his religious convictions. In King, it was indeed "often hard to tell where, if at all, the Christian substratum of his thought left off and the superstructure of his social theory began ... he was beyond question the most important Christian voice in the most important movement of social protest after World War II."[1]

Both Graham and King, something like iconic figures for modern American Protestantism, have come to represent the mainstream of Evangelical church life. The Evangelical tradition has proved remarkably resilient in modern America. But it is a tradition that has constantly outgrown its denominational boundaries. The main denominations of the Protestant heyday of the nineteenth century, the Methodists, Baptists, Presbyterians, and Congregationalists, have remained a significant presence. But they have ceded numbers increasingly to new alignments and new forms of ecclesial identity. Many of the new churches do not appear to aspire to the national (and even international) organization of the traditional denominations. Instead, they may be relatively localized, drawing members from a radius of thirty miles or so around the main church site. They may be founded by a single charismatic leader, or they may be perhaps the product of a schism within an existing church. Often they are, in effect, "house churches" that have outgrown the domestic setting. Some claim a following of thousands. Others may have no more than a couple of hundred members. They are in part the foundation of what has been called the "religious right," the coalition of conservative Protestant church people who have been particularly articulate as supporters of the Republican Party since the early 1980s.

But the history of Evangelicalism in the twentieth century has been complicated by two developments in particular. One is particularly difficult to identify, as it signifies rather a set of attitudes that may be encountered in many different churches. It is what is (almost always dismissively) called "Fundamentalism." At its most elementary level, the term is used commonly to mean simply a rigid, literal view of the authority of the Bible. But the term in this sense is mostly used pejoratively. The label "Fundamentalist" originally derived from the determination of a group of leading Evangelical church leaders to counter what they thought was the erosion of faith threatened by the growth of Modernism. Modernism was a movement of thought within Christianity that sought to adapt Christianity to modern ways of thinking, and in particular to the critical challenges scientific theory and historical argument had mounted against the Bible. Once again, in this history, the Bible is center stage, then. A series of booklets called *The Fundamentals: A Testimony to the Truth* (1910–15) defended the fundamentals or "basics" of the faith. But while the series rested on a general appeal to the truth of the "plain sense" of Scripture, it did not depend on an exclusive defense of the absolute, "literal" truth (that is, the assertion that the Bible is true in the exact sense in which it is written, as direct, recorded testimony of God, and to be taken only in that sense). That idea of "Fundamentalism" as a simple assumption of literal truth developed somewhat later, in particular at first among northern Baptists and Presbyterians in America. Its main target popularly came to be the teaching of the theory of evolution in schools. Its symbolic moment – the point ever since then popularly associated with Fundamentalism in America – came with the infamous "Scopes" trial in 1925, when the populist fundamentalist William Jennings Bryan opposed the lawyer Clarence Darrow in Dayton, Tennessee, who was defending a teacher called John Scopes who had taught evolution in the classroom. The trial eventually turned in Darrow's favor, and Bryan's ignorance of science and history was held up to ridicule. Nevertheless, the trial had highlighted the fundamentalist opposition to evolutionary theory, and served as a rallying call. From that time on, Fundamentalism has gathered momentum in Protestant America. It led to splits within the Baptist and Presbyterian churches in the 1920s and 1930s, and provoked the formation of new churches that have followed the conviction of literal authority much more self-consciously than their forebears. But, it must be emphasized, Fundamentalism in this more rigorous sense is a label that stretches across many denominations, and cannot always be distinguished neatly from a generally conservative theological position.

A similar confusion of labels arises from a consideration of the history of Pentecostalism, to which we must now turn. While there are certainly self-consciously "Pentecostalist" churches, there is also a sense in which a "charismatic revival," related to, and overlapping with Pentecostalism, has affected all of the mainstream Protestant denominations, and even extended to Catholicism. Moreover, some Pentecostalists and charismatics are also Fundamentalist, but many are not. Many Fundamentalists regard charismatics and Pentecostalists as dangerous innovators, who have risked replacing the authority of the Bible with an appeal to Spirit-filled experience. Yet charismatics and Pentecostalists are often themselves conservative in their views of personal and social morality, and also defenders of the plain sense of Scripture. In practical effect, they may appear to have a great deal in common with those who disavow the notion of spiritual gifts, and work alongside them in various campaigns. So the first great wave of revival in the western churches, the Evangelical revival, remains potent, but it has splintered at the same time. What is, however, increasingly clear about Pentecostalism is that its sheer scale – worldwide – is such that it is indeed possible to regard it as a third, continuing wave of renewal in its own right.

Pentecostalism in America

Pentecostalism began as a movement within black American Christianity, but it has spread to the white churches too. William J. Seymour (1870–1922) is usually credited as the first true Pentecostalist minister. In 1906 he took over a derelict Methodist church in Azusa Street in Los Angeles, and built up a congregation stressing the presence of the Holy Spirit. The signs of this were to become familiar among Pentecostalists – speaking in tongues, and miracle healings. There were, certainly, also familiar characteristics of the revivalism Seymour practiced, including hymn-singing, and highly charged and emotional preaching. Moreover, even the charismatic gifts of speaking in tongues and healings were not unique to the burgeoning Pentecostal movement. They can be traced back in Protestantism to the ferment of millenarian sects unleashed by the religious chaos of the English Civil Wars, when various ecstatic congregations for a time came into being, only to be suppressed. These kinds of emotional seizure resurfaced from time to time, particularly in early Methodism.

Methodism also bequeathed to the Pentecostal movement its emphasis on holiness, the notion that true believers, filled with the Holy Spirit, could be taken into a new relation with God even in this life, before death. Various churches in the late nineteenth century had been influenced by this teaching, including the Church of the Nazarene, founded in 1895 by Phineas F. Brese (1838–1916), a former Methodist minister. Pentecostalism in part was a development within this "holiness" movement. But it synthesized these elements of an older revivalist experience into a distinctive mix. In the past, ecstatic behavior had tended to be typical of times of unusual intensity and expectation, and had rarely been regarded as anything other than a temporary aberration. Ministers in particular had often been suspicious of this kind of behavior, fearing that it disrupted the good order that most congregations depended on for their survival and success. Now, it became a normal feature of the worship of these new churches. In other respects, their theology appeared comparable to Evangelicalism. Certainly, the Bible loomed just as large in the religious world-view of Pentecostalists as it did for other Evangelical Protestants. There was the same conviction of sinfulness and the need for repentance and conversion, and the same intense personal encounter with Jesus Christ. Study of Scripture was encouraged, as it was for other Evangelicals. Moral attitudes were much the same, too. But the twin doctrinal emphasis on the gifts of the Spirit and on the pursuit of holiness did slant this common Evangelical religion in a new direction. Pentecostalism appeared more optimistic than other forms of Evangelicalism. Spiritual gifts such as speaking in tongues did have some biblical justification. Paul in 1 Corinthians 12 speaks of "various kinds of tongues" as one of the gifts of the Spirit. Strictly speaking, Pentecostalists did not claim automatic authorization of tongues. Again following Paul, the gift of speaking in tongues had to be tested, to determine whether or not it was authentic. Nevertheless, in Pentecostal culture the manifestation of the gifts of the Spirit has often been seen as a sign of an individual's closeness to God, and this has been reinforced by the cultivation of the search for holiness. Corporately, this has fed a strong sense of closeness to God in Pentecostal churches. Paradoxically, it has often appealed especially to those who tend to see themselves as not part of the Christian mainstream – perhaps not part of the older, more traditional denominations, or part of the majority or historic church culture of an area. I say "paradoxically" here, because the energy and vitality of Pentecostalism has come close in some parts of the world precisely to turning it into the dominant church culture.

Pentecostalism is, accordingly, both closely identified with traditional

Pentecostalism made its most rapid and numerically significant inroads into black American Christianity

Evangelicalism, and yet definitely different in its spirit and practice. Its special gift has perhaps been a uniquely affirmative spirit, which has been exemplified in its ability to hold the attention of seemingly marginalized people by a strong conviction of their special relationship with God. It is not surprising, then, that Pentecostalism made its most rapid and numerically significant inroads into black American Christianity. But it branched out quickly to embrace various non-mainstream white Christian congregations. Many of these churches, black, white, and mixed race, came together in 1914 to form the Assemblies of God, the largest single Pentecostal denomination in America today. Pentecostalism was not free of the doctrinal disputes that have plagued other Christian traditions, however. An early dispute over Trinitarian belief – that is, in effect, over God's "threeness," and particularly over whether or not Jesus was divine – forced a division within the Assemblies of God in 1916, leading to the formation of a breakaway "Unitarian" Pentecostal group. A more damaging division occurred over the issue of race, with southern Pentecostal churches in particular eventually finding it impossible to sustain mixed race congregations. Distinct white Pentecostal denominations, including the Church of God and the Pentecostal Holiness Church, came into being. For several generations even this new and exciting development within the Christian church, for all its dazzling vitality and sense of an immediacy of each Christian's belonging to God, could not altogether shut out the impact of one of the most controversial and divisive issues in American society.

Yet by the 1970s the most acute divisions over race had largely been exorcised. Pentecostalism had settled into a dramatic and continuing rise in membership, overshadowing many of the older Protestant denominations. Between 1940 and 1988 the various churches represented in the Assemblies of God rose from around 199,000 members to over two million, a growth rate of almost 1,000%. The churches represented in the Christian and Missionary Alliance historically have distanced themselves from Pentecostalism, but they share many characteristics with Pentecostals, including a holiness doctrine. They rose by just over 700% from 23,000 members in 1940 to 260,000 in 1988. Current estimates of the actual number of people attending Pentecostal churches in America today suggest that the figure may be as high as twenty million. Compared with the total numbers of Roman Catholics, Baptists, and Methodists, these numbers remain relatively small, but the growth rates may indicate future trends. In the same period, Roman Catholics increased by 158%, Southern Baptists by 199%, and Methodists by just 13%. Pentecostalism, in terms of numbers, is not yet a dominant presence in America, but it is a vociferous, distinct, and fast-growing part of Christianity. And its influence may well be under-represented in these figures, since it has effected and encouraged the formation of Pentecostal or charismatic wings within many of the older denominations.

Pentecostalism in Britain

For reasons that are difficult to fathom, Pentecostalism has never had quite the impact in Britain that it has had in America. Some have suggested that this is because British society, like that of other countries in western Europe, has passed through a time of conflict over the dominance of a particular established church, and has become something of a secularized society. Certainly, churchgoing as a whole is much lower in Britain today than is the case in America. There is endless controversy over the accuracy of the relevant figures, but regular church attendance in Britain probably rests somewhere between 5% and 10% of the population. In America, the figure would appear to be nearer 40%, according to some surveys. One has to go back to the mid-nineteenth century to encounter anything comparable in Britain. Moreover, although it is common in Britain now to talk of a "post-Christian" situation, and there are even overseas Christian missionaries working in Britain today, nevertheless the fact that Britain has a long history of Christian faith ironically may present a positive handicap to those seeking the re-evangelization of British society. Pentecostals have drawn much attention and some support – considerably so in the inner cities – but mostly through the growth of immigrant communities since the Second World War.

Early Pentecostal churches in Britain came into existence near the beginning of the twentieth century. A great revival in Welsh Protestantism from 1904 to 1906 proved to be the background to the emergence of a number of Pentecostal churches. The Elim Pentecostal Church, for example, was founded in 1915 by George Jeffreys (1889–1972), a product of the Welsh revival. It has grown into a worldwide church, with over 9,000 congregations across the world. Its largest church in Britain today is the Kensington Temple in London, which claims to be in touch with 15,000 members and has embraced the cell-church method of growth, by which large, single assemblies are avoided as a regular means of worship in favor of an expanding number of smaller, personal churches. The Apostolic Church was another example, again founded in 1916 as an indirect result of the Welsh revival. Again, it has led to the foundation of Pentecostal churches across the world. These were originally, it should be emphasized, almost entirely white churches. They drew on an existing tradition of Evangelical conviction and revivalist fervor, and on an inherited (if sometimes dormant) perception that particular gifts such as speaking in tongues and prophecy might very well be signs of the indwelling of the Holy Spirit in the life of a believer.

Pentecostalism in Britain today has been particularly fed by the formation of churches associated with immigrant communities. The Assemblies of God have flourished in Britain, for example, with predominantly Afro-Caribbean congregations in the cities. African churches, catering for distinct West and East African congregations, have also sometimes taken a Pentecostal form. There have even been Korean and Philippine Pentecostal churches formed in British cities. These are all, almost without exception, robust and growing – if overall still relatively small – sectors of the churchgoing community.

Yet to describe the rise of Pentecostalism in Britain in this way is not to exhaust the range of its influence. For it has overlapped with a movement in the mainstream denominations that has also emphasized the gifts of the Spirit, namely the charismatic movement. Charismatic churches, sometimes altogether detached from the traditional churches, began to appear on the British religious scene particularly in the 1960s and 1970s. Even in the established Church of England a strong charismatic wing emerged. The Fountain Trust, founded in 1964, exists to encourage charismatic gifts in the Church of England. David Watson, Vicar of St Michael-le-Belfry in York and then of Holy Trinity, Brompton, in London, became a noted charismatic preacher and evangelist. Holy Trinity, Brompton was also the main site for a manifestation of the "Toronto blessing," a charismatic experience which threw those undergoing the experience onto the ground in something like hysteria, in the late 1990s. Anglican charismatics, alongside charismatics in the Methodist, United Reformed, and even the Roman Catholic churches, have often been ecumenical in spirit, prepared to work alongside other Christians. Yet there are separatist churches, too, particularly among the Baptists, the Brethren, and the many small independent churches. These churches have disavowed contact with other Christians, and have concentrated exclusively on their own growth. Though mostly small, they appear to be growing substantially, and are often contrasted with the mainstream churches, which are still undergoing contraction.

A worldwide renewal?

The most compelling evidence that the Pentecostal movement, and the associated phenomenon of the charismatic revival, represents a distinct, third "wave" of renewal in the modern Church comes, however, neither from Britain nor America, but from the extraordinary growth of Pentecostalism in the "Third" world. This has been most remarkable in Latin America. Latin America has long been a continent of immense Roman Catholic dominance. The appearance of Pentecostal churches in parts of the continent early in the twentieth century can hardly have attracted much attention, they were so small. The Methodist Pentecostal Church in Chile arose in 1909 out of a clash between what had fast become an indigenous and unrestrained Chilean Methodist revivalism, and the more educated and restrained attitude of North American missionaries. The Chileans in effect took over their church, and declared themselves separate from the official Methodist church of Chile. The latter struggled to grow, but the former made rapid strides to over a million members by the end of the twentieth century. In Brazil, before the twentieth century modest Protestant churches were already in existence – Baptists and Presbyterians in particular. These experienced some growth early in the century, deepening into more rapid advance under the impact of Pentecostalism later in the century. One scholar has noted the tendency of these new and growing Pentecostal churches to attract a wider racial mix than the longer-established Catholic churches, and also the attraction of the Protestant churches' emphasis on individual, personal interpretation of the Bible, and on the involvement of their members in the running of their own churches.[2] There may now be as many as 14 million Pentecostals in Brazil. Overall, it is estimated that something like 33 million people in Latin America are now members of Pentecostal or charismatic Protestant churches.

The story in Africa is not all that different in summary, though the history of Africa – its colonization over several centuries by rival European states, its late de-colonization, and its wars – is perhaps more complex still. One estimate is that there are now over 40 million members of Pentecostal or charismatic churches in Africa as a whole. Many of these belong to independent churches, often of immense size in their own right. The Redeemed Christian Church of God (RCCG) was founded in Nigeria in 1952, by Josiah Akindayomi, a former convert from the Yoruba religion to Anglicanism, who had subsequently joined the Cherubim and Seraphim Church, an independent church. The RCCG is based in Lagos, but now has over 2,000 parishes in Nigeria, and has founded many others in neighboring countries. It is just one of the countless independent Pentecostal churches that have appeared in Africa in the last fifty years or so.

A similar story can again be told of the Far East, where Pentecostalism again has made significant inroads, both in the "modernized" societies of South Korea and Taiwan, and in Indonesia and China. Numbers here, particularly in China, are hard to estimate, but certainly run into the millions.

Why is this new and energetic form of Protestantism making so much headway throughout the world? The answer that Pentecostals would presumably give is that it is because the Lord's Spirit is at work in the world. The growth of these churches is evidence of his power. He is gathering in the nations before a final consummation of history and his coming again. We do not have to question that explanation, if we wish not to do so, but we can add some more mundane observations. Like the revivalism of an earlier age, Pentecostalism is immensely flexible. Its informal, tradition-free nature enables it to flourish in many different contexts. It does not require financial investment to found a church – any building large enough to hand will do. It does not require the close supervision of a ministerial hierarchy – its organization is mostly local, and often independent. Though it places great emphasis on its preachers, it is in other ways remarkably democratic. Its members are drawn into exercising financial and practical responsibility for their own church. Its worship is often noisy, and immensely joyful, and therefore equally suitable for families as for single people. Through gospel choirs, music groups, and choruses and worship songs, it has found a medium that appeals to the growing international popular culture emanating chiefly from America. Moreover, its theology is both practical and reassuring. It shares the Protestant conviction that every man and woman is his or her own interpreter of the Bible. It encourages its followers to live in the world of the Bible by regular reading, making its stories and people familiar, and bringing its message to bear on every aspect of their lives. It projects and supports definite moral values, and demands restraint and sacrifice from its members – as do all the world's great religions. But it also offers the possibility that believers may experience confirmation of God's grace at work in their lives, by the gifts of the Spirit, or by miraculous healings.

Some have argued that, for all these reasons, Pentecostalism has particularly appealed to people facing the pressure of economic and social modernization. Pentecostalism requires a certain level of literacy, they have argued, but not too much – enough to read the Bible, not enough to widen one's education to encompass the critical disciplines that may have eroded the authority of the Bible in the affluent West. They have also argued that it has made each follower the master of his or her own destiny, giving them the responsibility for exercising choice about their lifestyles, at the same time as attributing the outcome of these decisions to the hand of God. Such arguments are difficult to substantiate, however, because they do not seem to capture the complexity of individual believers' experience, nor the complexity of particular churches' histories. But they do at least point to some of the ambiguities of this third great wave of Christian renewal. From the perspective of a western skeptic, Pentecostalism looks like an extraordinary throwback to a pre-modern past. Its ecstatic religious behavior shares much in common with early modern revivalism. Its conviction of physical manifestations of God's Spirit, and of the possibility of miraculous healing, does not appear to fit very well with a technological and scientific understanding. Yet many Pentecostalists themselves do not feel the tension at all. They are able to combine living in a "modern" society, using modern technology, with the Spirit-filled universe of Pentecostal Christianity without apparent difficulty. The ambiguities of Pentecostalism and its relationship with the modern world are also evident in the experience of women. Sharing a conservative understanding of women's ministry – that is to say, ceding leadership of congregations to men, following a literal reading of Paul's view of male authority in the Letter to the Ephesians – Pentecostal churches are almost invariably led by male pastors. Yet women have a great deal of influence in Pentecostal churches, often leading choirs, forming and leading other groups, and as pastors' wives sharing openly in their husbands' ministry. In this respect, of course, Pentecostalism is not significantly different from other conservative forms of Protestantism. But its ability to absorb the apparent contradiction of traditional belief and modern values and roles is evident, all the same.

Is Pentecostalism the shape of the Christian future, then? It is not at all clear that the rising trajectory of Pentecostal growth is anywhere near an end. If it seems at present unlikely that, in America and Britain, the Pentecostal churches will expand to such an extent that they finally overtake the older denominations, nevertheless they are clearly set to be a major, dynamic element of church life in these countries for years to come. No one can tell what their impact on American and British society overall will be, but we can be sure that it has yet to reveal its fullest extent. There are some signs in Britain that Pentecostal churches are beginning to work collaboratively with the older denominations, and the same has been true in America for quite a while. Yet Pentecostal Christianity does have a distinct identity, and perhaps a distinct role. It may well influence the pattern of worship, organization, and belonging in the older denominations in ways no one can yet predict. Elsewhere in the world, its influence may also yet run deeper still.

1 Noll, *A History of Christianity in the United States and Canada*, p. 507.

2 D. Martin, *Tongues of Fire. The Explosion of Protestantism in Latin America* (Oxford: Blackwell, 1990), p. 71.

CONCLUSION

THE STORY OF revivalism in the modern world has taken us across a very diverse range of Christian churches over the last three hundred years. We have seen how the fundamental division in western Christianity opened up by the Reformation broadened into two different church cultures, Protestant and Catholic, and how successive waves of popular renewal have worked their way through these two kinds of Christian belonging to transform them. All churches risk becoming passive and inert if they do not find the means to renew themselves over time. Christianity has a long history, and has had to rediscover (and some would say reinvent) itself many times in order to survive. If modern revivalism in the specialized sense, with its appeal to mass meetings, its unashamed exploitation of technology and of organization, and its heady emotional message, has helped the churches to adapt and survive in the sometimes anti-religious climate of modern society, then its value – under the Gospel – is unquestionable. This popular revivalism has been a thread of continuity running through modern church history, from older Protestant denominations such as Anglicans and Episcopalians, through to the newer churches of the revival itself, the Methodists, and on even to Roman Catholicism, and then latterly to Pentecostalism. Yet we have also seen how it has changed subtly, according to the different church contexts in which it thrived. It has attracted suspicion as well as support. It has burned brightly in periods of special intensity, and then died away. It has flowed over into a general influence running through all of these denominations, so that even those churches that self-consciously tried to stand aloof from it – such as Anglo-Catholic churches – have indirectly or unconsciously been affected by it. It is by no means the only possible way in which Christianity can sustain itself in the modern world, but it is perhaps by far the most energetic and currently effective way. Its history is precisely that – a story of Christianity's adaptation to the challenges thrown at it by the modern world.

Thus, the present of the churches with which we are familiar today has been formed by their past. And yet their history shows us that, at all times, Christians have labored ceaselessly to understand what their faith is demanding of them in the circumstances in which they have found themselves. At the very center of this restless, continuous exploration of what it means to be a Christian today, has lain the Bible. Sometimes it has moved squarely into focus in this narrative, as we have seen how different groups used the Bible to justify or to criticize particular aspects of church life. At other times, it has moved into the background. Yet it has always been the very starting-point of Christian self-understanding. Protestants went to the Bible to rediscover for themselves the truth of justification through faith alone. Catholics saw in the Bible the grounding for their ministerial hierarchy, and the authority of the papacy. In time, Anglicans divided over how to apply the Bible to the Church, with some claiming they needed to "purify" the Church to conform it to the biblical model, and others suggesting that there was no definitive biblical model of the Church, and that God had given his people freedom to order the Church as they saw fit. Methodists in time found the inspiration for the doctrine of final perseverance, and the pursuit of holiness, in the Bible. Pentecostalists saw the proof of the operation of God's Spirit in his works in the Bible – and if they could be traced in the Bible, why could they not happen today?

It is tempting to adopt the superior tone of an aloof historian, and to suggest that the Bible has always, and will always, generate diverse interpretations, no one of which can be shown to be better intrinsically than any other. But that would not do justice to the passion and conviction with which all of these diverse churches, participants in these periodic renewals, have sought to discern the shape of true discipleship in applying the Bible to their own day. It would not do justice, either, to the real elements of commonalty underlying the Christian experience over the centuries. Through this complex history, Christians have been a people of the book. The Bible has shaped their lives. It has formed beliefs, and organizations, at times bewildering in their differences. But it has always held before Christians the central truth of Christ, and of his sacrificial death. Just as history has disclosed to us the diversity of Christian experience, so it has also demonstrated the abiding conviction of Christians everywhere that their lives could take significance only in the light of what God has done in Jesus Christ. This is the conviction that has embedded itself in human institutions and practices, and then broken free of them again when it seemed that they were threatening to stifle it. This is the conviction that has inspired revival.

Bibliography

This cannot be a fully comprehensive bibliography, as the books and articles on this subject are vast in number. I have listed here only what I have consulted specifically for this book. Many of the works of the great revivalist preachers of the past, and of the Reformers, are now available on the worldwide web. In a few places in the text, I have used websites and listed the addresses in the references. Here, I have provided details of comparable published editions.

Bettenson, H. (ed.), *Documents of the Christian Church* (Oxford University Press, 1943).

Blumhoffer, E. L., *Restoring the Faith. The Assemblies of God, Pentecostalism, and American Culture* (Urbana and Chicago: University of Illinois Press, 1993).

Bossy, J., *The English Catholic Community 1570–1850* (London: DLT, 1975).

Brown, S. J., *The National Churches of England, Ireland and Scotland 1801–1846* (Oxford University Press, 2001).

Bruce, S., *God is Dead. Secularization in the West* (Oxford: Blackwell, 2002).

Clements, K., *Faith on the Frontier. A Life of J. H. Oldham* (Edinburgh: T & T Clark, 1999).

Cragg, G. R., *The Church in the Age of Reason 1648–1789* (Harmondsworth: Penguin, 1960).

Dolan, J. P., *Catholic Revivalism. The American Experience 1830–1900* (University of Notre Dame Press, 1978).

Edwards, Jonathan, *The Sermons of Jonathan Edwards: a Reader* (ed. W. H. Kimnach, K. P. Minkema, and D. A. Sweeney, *New Haven, Connecticut*: Yale University Press, 1999).

Edwards, M., 'John Wesley', in R. Davies and G. Rupp (eds.), *A History of the Methodist Church in Great Britain, Vol. 1* (London: Epworth, 1965).

Findlay, J. F., Dwight L. Moody. *American Evangelist 1837–1899* (University of Chicago Press, 1969).

Finke, R. and Stark, R., '*How the Upstart Sects Won America: 1776–1850*', Journal for the Scientific Study of Religion, 28 (1989).

Handy, R. T., A Christian America. *Protestant Hopes and Historical Realities* (Oxford University Press, 1984).

Hardman, K. J., *Charles Grandison Finney 1792–1875* (New York: Syracuse University Press, 1987).

Harris, H., *Fundamentalism and Evangelicals* (Oxford: Clarendon, 1998).

Harris, R., Lourdes. *Body and Spirit in the Secular Age* (Allen Lane, London, 1999).

Kent, J., *Holding the Fort. Studies in Victorian Revivalism* (London: Epworth, 1978).

Kent, J., *Wesley and the Wesleyans. Religion in Eighteenth-Century Britain* (Cambridge University Press, 2002).

Lincoln, C. E. and Mamiya, L. H., *The Black Church in the African American Experience* (Durham, NC: Duke University Press, 1990).

Luther, Martin, *To the Christian Nobility of the German Nation, in Three Treatises* (Philadelphia: Fortress Press, 1970).

Luther, Martin, *The Bondage of the Will* (London: James Clarke, 1957).

McGrath, A. E and Marks, D. C., *The Blackwell Companion to Protestantism* (Oxford: Blackwell, 2004).

McLeod, D. H., *Religion and the People of Western Europe 1789–1970* (Oxford University Press, 1981).

McLoughlin, W. G., *Revivals, Awakenings and Reform: an Essay on Religion and Social Change in America, 1607–1977* (Chicago: University of Chicago Press, 1978).

Martin, D., *Tongues of Fire. The Explosion of Protestantism in Latin America* (Oxford: Blackwell, 1990).

Neill, S., *A History of Christian Missions* (Harmondsworth: Penguin, 1964).

Noll, M. A., *A History of Christianity in the United States and Canada* (London: SPCK, 1992).

Percy, M., Words, *Wonders and Power. Understanding Contemporary Christian Fundamentalism and Revivalism* (London: SPCK, 1996).

Rack, H. D., *Reasonable Enthusiast. John Wesley and the Rise of Methodism* (London: Epworth, 1989).

Smith, T. L., *Revivalism and Social Reform in Mid-Nineteenth Century America* (New York: Abingdon Press, 1957).

Southey, R., *Life of Wesley* (London: Frederick Warne, new ed., 1889).

Sperry, W. L., *Religion in America* (Cambridge University Press, 1945).

Synan, V., *The Holiness Pentecostal Movement in the United States* (Grand Rapids, Michigan: Eerdmans, 1971).

William Tyndale's Old Testament (ed. D. Daniell, New Haven: Yale University Press, 1992).

Vidler, A. R., *The Church in an Age of Revolution* (Harmondsworth: Penguin, 1961).

Wakefield, G., '*John and Charles Wesley: A Tale of Two Brothers*', in G. Rowell (ed.), *The English Religious Tradition and the Genius of Anglicanism* (Wantage: Ikon, 1992).

Walsh, J. D., '*The Origins of the Evangelical Revival*', in G. V. Bennett and J. D. Walsh, Essays in Modern Church History (London: A & C Black, 1966).

Walsh, J. D., '*Methodism at the end of the eighteenth century*', in R. Davies and G. Rupp (eds.), *A History of the Methodist Church in Great Britain, Vol. 1* (London: Epworth, 1965).

Ward, W. R., *Faith and Faction* (Epworth, London, 1993).

Whitefield, George, *Select sermons (with an account of his life by J. C. Ryle and a summary of his doctrine by R. Elliot, Edinburgh*: Banner of Truth Trust, 1958).

INDEX